Better Homes and Gardens®

salads

COOKING FOR TODAY

BETTER HOMES AND GARDENS® BOOKS
Des Moines

BETTER HOMES AND GARDENS® BOOKS
An Imprint of Meredith® Books
President, Book Group: Joseph J. Ward
Vice President and Editorial Director: Elizabeth P. Rice
Executive Editor: Nancy N. Green
Managing Editor: Christopher Cavanaugh
Art Director: Ernest Shelton
Test Kitchen Director: Sharon Stilwell

SALADS
Editor: Mary Major Williams
Writer: Linda Henry
Associate Art Director: Tom Wegner
Graphic Production Coordinator: Paula Forest
Production Manager: Doug Johnston
Test Kitchen Product Supervisor: Marilyn Cornelius
Food Stylists: Lynn Blanchard, Janet Pittman, Jennifer Peterson
Photographers: Mike Dieter, Scott Little
Cover Photographer: Andy Lyons

On the cover: Chicken and Fruit Plates with Honey-Jalepeño Dressing (see recipe, page 57)

Meredith Corporation Corporate Officers:
Chairman of the Executive Committee: E. T. Meredith III
Chairman of the Board, President and Chief Executive Officer: Jack D. Rehm
Group Presidents: Joseph J. Ward, Books; William T. Kerr, Magazines; Philip A. Jones, Broadcasting;
    Allen L. Sabbag, Real Estate
Vice Presidents: Leo R. Armatis, Corporate Relations; Thomas G. Fisher, General Counsel and Secretary;
    Larry D. Hartsook, Finance; Michael A. Sell, Treasurer; Kathleen J. Zehr, Controller and Assistant Secretary

WE CARE!

All of us at Better Homes and Gardens® Books are dedicated to providing you with the information
and ideas you need to create tasty foods. We welcome your comments and suggestions. Write us at:
Better Homes and Gardens® Books, Cookbook Editorial Department, 1716 Locust St., Des Moines,
IA 50309-3023

Our seal assures you that every recipe in *Salads* has been
tested in the Better Homes and Gardens® Test Kitchen.
This means that each recipe is practical and reliable, and
meets our high standards of taste appeal. We guarantee
your satisfaction with this book for as long as you own it.

Salad days are here! Although at one time that meant we could only enjoy a delectable salad during the summer months, we now have a boundless array of the freshest greens, veggies, fruits, and herbs at our fingertips year-round.

This book contains mostly main-dish salads, along with a few side-dish salads. Some are accented with exciting new flavors from around the world; while others are tried-and-true family favorites.

In all the salads, we've used imagination and creativity to capture a refreshing variety of enticing flavors and textures. As you'll discover, there's no end to the possible combinations of ingredients. You'll find pork mixed with black beans and corn for a southwestern fiesta, while curry, grapes, and mandarin oranges add pizzazz to chicken salad. Even tuna and pasta are given a new flavor with an herb-and-mustard dressing. On the following pages you'll find more sensational salads—each one, an eating adventure.

CONTENTS

SELECTING SALAD GREENS

Here's a quick rundown of the salad greens used in recipes throughout this book:

Boston or Bibb lettuce: Butterhead varieties. Small, loosely packed leaves. Subtly sweet, buttery flavor.

Chinese cabbage: Elongated, tightly packed, ruffly leaves with wide stalks. Mild, sweet flavor.

Iceberg lettuce: Compact, smooth, round head with crisp leaves that vary from pale to medium green. Mild, watery flavor.

Leaf lettuce: Sprawling, curly, crisp, yet tender leaves. Sweet, delicate flavor.

Mesclun: Mixture of piquant, delicate baby lettuces.

Radicchio: Ruby-red leaves with thick, white veins that form a small, round, compact head. Slightly bitter and peppery tasting.

Romaine: Large, elongated, sturdy leaves that branch from a white base. Slightly sharp flavor.

Spinach: Crinkled or smooth-textured leaves with long stems. Somewhat earthy flavor.

Salad savoy: Large, frilly leaves that can be purple, creamy white, pink, or green. Cabbage-like flavor.

Watercress: Small, round, delicate leaves on edible stems. Peppery flavor.

HANDLING SALAD GREENS

*Remove and discard any bruised, discolored, tough, or wilted leaves.

*Wash greens thoroughly by rinsing them under cold running water or swishing the leaves through a water-filled sink. (Spinach leaves are usually especially sandy and may require several changes of water.)

*Dry greens thoroughly before storing them. Place them on several layers of paper towels or use a salad spinner.

*Wrap the dry greens in dry paper towels (or kitchen towels) before placing them in a plastic bag or airtight container. Greens generally stay crisp for three to four days.

*Tear, rather than cut, leaves to avoid bruising and browning. Cut greens only when the recipe calls for shredding.

*When adding salad dressings to tossed green salads, remember:
1. Add dressing only to greens that are thoroughly dry. (The dressing gets diluted otherwise.)
2. Add dressing just before serving (unless the recipe states otherwise) to avoid damp, soggy salads.
3. Add only enough dressing to lightly coat the salad greens.

*Toss salads in large salad bowls with two salad servers or spoons. Gently push downward to the bottom of the bowl with both salad servers and lift up and over.

MARINATED GREEK STEAK SALAD

Radicchio, an Italian chicory with bright red leaves and white veins, adds a colorful accent and peppery taste to this salad masterpiece.

12	ounces boneless beef sirloin steak, cut 1 inch thick
1	14-ounce can artichoke hearts, drained and cut into quarters
½	of a medium red onion, sliced and separated into rings
¼	cup Greek olives *or* pitted ripe olives
⅓	cup olive oil *or* salad oil
3	tablespoons red wine vinegar
2	tablespoons lemon juice
1	tablespoon snipped fresh oregano *or* 1 teaspoon dried oregano, crushed
1	tablespoon anchovy paste
¼	teaspoon pepper
2	large cloves garlic, minced
3	cups torn romaine *or* spinach
3	cups torn leaf lettuce *or* iceberg lettuce
1	cup torn radicchio *or* red-tip leaf lettuce
2	medium tomatoes, cut into wedges
½	cup crumbled feta cheese (2 ounces)

Slash fatty edges of steak at 1-inch intervals, being careful not to cut into the meat. Place the steak on the unheated rack of a broiler pan. Broil 3 inches from the heat for 6 minutes. Turn steak. Broil to desired doneness (allow 6 to 8 minutes more for medium). Cool slightly. Cut into thin slices. Place meat in a deep bowl along with artichoke hearts, onion, and olives.

For marinade, in a screw-top jar combine oil, vinegar, lemon juice, oregano, anchovy paste, pepper, and garlic. Cover and shake well. Pour marinade over meat mixture. Cover and marinate in the refrigerator for 6 to 24 hours, stirring occasionally.

In a large mixing bowl combine romaine or spinach, leaf lettuce or iceberg lettuce, and radicchio or red-tip leaf lettuce. Line four salad plates with the mixed greens. Top with meat mixture. Arrange tomato wedges around meat mixture. Sprinkle with feta cheese. Makes 4 servings.

Nutrition information per serving: 444 calories, 28 g protein, 18 g carbohydrate, 31 g fat (8 g saturated), 74 mg cholesterol, 713 mg sodium, 970 mg potassium.

HEARTY BEEF SALAD WITH HORSERADISH DRESSING

In the summertime, grill the sirloin steak for this tasty salad. Place the meat on a grill rack over medium coals. Grill, uncovered, for 16 to 20 minutes for rare or 20 to 24 minutes for medium.

  8 ounces green beans
1½ cups baby carrots
12 ounces beef sirloin steak, cut 1 inch
       thick
  4 cups torn Boston *or* Bibb lettuce
  1 16-ounce can julienne beets, rinsed
       and drained
     Horseradish Dressing
     Cracked black pepper (optional)

Wash green beans; remove ends and strings. Cut beans in half crosswise. In a covered, medium saucepan cook beans in boiling water for 5 minutes. Add baby carrots and cook for 10 to 15 minutes more or till vegetables are tender; drain. Cover and chill for 4 to 24 hours.

Place steak on the unheated rack of a broiler pan. Broil 3 inches from the heat for 8 to 12 minutes for rare or 13 to 17 minutes for medium. Slice steak across the grain into thin slices.

Divide torn lettuce among four salad plates. Arrange green beans, baby carrots, steak slices, and beets atop lettuce. Pass the Horseradish Dressing. Sprinkle each serving with cracked black pepper, if desired. Makes 4 servings.

Horseradish Dressing: In a small mixing bowl beat together ½ of a 3-ounce package *cream cheese,* softened, and 2 tablespoons *horseradish sauce.* Stir in enough *milk* (3 to 4 tablespoons) to make dressing of drizzling consistency. Chill till serving time. (Dressing will thicken slightly if made ahead and chilled.)

Nutrition information per serving: 360 calories, 32 g protein, 24 g carbohydrate, 15 g fat (6 g saturated), 94 mg cholesterol, 497 mg sodium, 1,078 mg potassium.

STEAK AND PASTA SALAD WITH PEANUT-PEPPER DRESSING

Look for lemongrass, a lemon-flavored herb resembling a green onion, in Oriental food shops, farmer's markets, or some grocery stores.

4   ounces fine noodles *or* fusilli pasta, broken (2½ cups)
⅓   cup rice wine vinegar *or* vinegar
⅓   cup salad oil
3   tablespoons soy sauce
2   tablespoons peanut butter
1   tablespoon chopped fresh lemongrass *or* snipped fresh cilantro
2   cloves garlic, minced
¼   teaspoon crushed red pepper
1   pound boneless beef top sirloin steak, cut 1 inch thick
5   cups shredded Chinese cabbage, spinach, romaine, *and/or* bok choy
½   cup shredded carrot
4   green onions, cut lengthwise into fourths and bias-sliced into 1-inch pieces
½   medium cucumber, sliced
1   medium yellow summer squash, halved lengthwise and sliced
¼   cup chopped peanuts
    Sliced red hot peppers (optional)

Cook noodles or pasta according to package directions; drain. Rinse pasta and drain again. Chill.

For dressing, in a blender container or food processor bowl combine vinegar, oil, soy sauce, peanut butter, lemongrass or cilantro, garlic, and crushed red pepper. Cover and blend or process till combined.

Trim fat from meat. Place meat in a shallow dish. Pour *1/3 cup* of the dressing over meat; turn once. Cover and marinate in the refrigerator for 2 hours. Chill remaining dressing.

Drain meat, discarding marinade. Place meat on the unheated rack of a broiler pan. Broil 3 inches from heat for 12 to 15 minutes for medium doneness, turning once.

Meanwhile, in a mixing bowl combine chilled noodles or pasta; Chinese cabbage, spinach, romaine, and/or bok choy; carrot; and green onions. Add *¼ cup* of the remaining dressing. Toss to coat.

Arrange noodle mixture on four salad plates. Cut warm meat into thin strips. Place meat on the noodle mixture. Arrange cucumber and squash around the noodle mixture. Drizzle with remaining dressing. Sprinkle with chopped peanuts. Garnish each serving with sliced hot peppers, if desired. Makes 4 servings.

Nutrition information per serving: 580 calories, 36 g protein, 32 g carbohydrate, 36 g fat (7 g saturated), 102 mg cholesterol, 873 mg sodium, 845 mg potassium.

STIR-FRIED BEEF AND SHIITAKE MUSHROOM SALAD

Shiitake (shih TOCK ee) mushrooms are brown Oriental mushrooms with large, floppy caps and a rich, meaty flavor. Look for them in Oriental grocery stores or the produce section of large grocery stores.

12 ounces boneless beef sirloin steak *or* pork tenderloin, cut into thin bite-size strips
1   8-ounce bottle (1 cup) oil-and-vinegar salad dressing
2   tablespoons dry sherry
2   tablespoons soy sauce
1   tablespoon brown sugar
1   clove garlic, minced
⅛   teaspoon ground ginger
12 cups torn mixed greens
1½ cups sliced fresh shiitake *or* other mushrooms
½   cup sliced green onions
1   tablespoon olive oil *or* cooking oil
1   large red sweet pepper, cut into thin strips

Place meat in a plastic bag set in a deep bowl. For marinade, in a small bowl stir together salad dressing, sherry, soy sauce, brown sugar, garlic, and ginger; pour over steak. Close bag. Marinate in the refrigerator for 6 hours or overnight, turning bag occasionally.

In a large bowl toss together mixed greens, mushrooms, and green onions. Divide greens mixture among six salad plates. Set aside.

Drain meat, reserving ⅔ *cup* of the marinade. Preheat a wok or large skillet over high heat; add oil. (Add more oil as necessary during cooking.) Stir-fry sweet pepper in hot oil for 2 minutes or till crisp-tender. Remove pepper from wok. Add meat to hot wok. Stir-fry for 2 to 3 minutes or to desired doneness. Add reserved marinade and sweet pepper to wok. Cook and stir till boiling.

To serve, spoon the hot meat mixture over greens mixture on salad plates. Serve immediately. Makes 6 servings.

Nutrition information per serving: 265 calories, 16 g protein, 9 g carbohydrate, 19 g fat (3 g saturated), 36 mg cholesterol, 666 mg sodium, 654 mg potassium.

THAI BEEF SALAD

Refreshing mint, salty fish sauce, tart lime, hot red pepper, and a little sweetness—all the flavors Thais love are brought together in this one salad, known as yam neua.

4   cups torn mixed greens
⅓   cup fresh whole mint leaves *or* cilantro leaves
2   tablespoons snipped fresh mint *or* cilantro
2   tablespoons lime juice
4   teaspoons fish sauce (nam pla) *or* soy sauce
2   teaspoons sugar
¼   teaspoon ground red pepper
1   tablespoon peanut oil *or* cooking oil
1   pound boneless beef top round steak, cut into thin, bite-size strips
2   medium tomatoes, cut into wedges
1   medium cucumber, halved lengthwise and sliced
3   green onions, bias sliced into 1-inch pieces

Divide greens among four salad plates; set aside. For dressing, in a large mixing bowl stir together the ⅓ cup whole mint or cilantro leaves, the 2 tablespoons snipped mint or cilantro, lime juice, fish sauce or soy sauce, sugar, and ground red pepper. Set aside.

In a wok or large skillet heat peanut oil or cooking oil over medium-high heat. Add *half* of the beef to the wok or skillet. Stir-fry for 2 to 3 minutes or till desired doneness. Remove beef. Stir-fry remaining beef. Return all the beef to the wok or skillet; heat through.

Add the warm beef, tomatoes, cucumber, and green onions to the dressing. Toss lightly to mix. Divide beef mixture among greens on salad plates. Serve immediately. Makes 4 servings.

Nutrition information per serving: 244 calories, 29 g protein, 11 g carbohydrate, 9 g fat (2 g saturated), 72 mg cholesterol, 364 mg sodium, 812 mg potassium.

TACO SALAD

A tomatillo (tohm ah TEE oh) looks like a small green tomato, but has a thin, parchmentlike covering (that is removed before cooking.) The flavor is a combination of lemon, apple, and herbs. Look for tomatillos in the produce section of your supermarket.

Tortilla Cups
Tomatillo Guacamole
8 ounces lean ground beef
3 cloves garlic, minced
1 15-ounce can dark red kidney beans, rinsed and drained
¾ cup frozen whole kernel corn
1 8-ounce jar taco sauce
1 tablespoon chili powder
8 cups torn leaf lettuce *or* iceberg lettuce
2 medium tomatoes, chopped
1 large green pepper, chopped
¾ cup shredded sharp cheddar cheese (3 ounces)
4 green onions, thinly sliced

Prepare Tortilla Cups; set aside. Prepare Tomatillo Guacamole; chill.

In a medium skillet cook ground beef and garlic till beef is brown. Drain off fat. Stir in kidney beans, corn, taco sauce, and chili powder. Bring to boiling. Reduce heat. Cover and simmer for 10 minutes.

Meanwhile, in a large bowl combine lettuce, tomatoes, green pepper, cheddar cheese, and green onions.

To serve, divide the lettuce mixture among the Tortilla Cups. Top each with some of the beef mixture and the Tomatillo Guacamole. Makes 6 servings.

Tortilla Cups: Lightly brush six *9- or 10-inch flour tortillas* with a small amount of water or spray *nonstick spray coating* onto one side of each tortilla. Spray nonstick coating into six small oven-safe bowls or 16-ounce individual casseroles. Press tortillas, coated sides up, into bowls or casseroles. Place a ball of foil in each tortilla cup to help hold its shape. Bake in a 350° oven for 15 to 20 minutes or till light brown. Remove foil; cool. Remove Tortilla Cups from bowls. Serve immediately or store in an airtight container for up to five days.

Tomatillo Guacamole: Rinse, drain, and finely chop 4 canned *tomatillos* (about ⅓ cup). *Or,* simmer 2 husked tomatillos (about 3½ ounces) in boiling water for 10 minutes; drain and chop. In a small mixing bowl combine tomatillos; ½ of a small seeded, peeled, and chopped *avocado* (about ½ cup); 2 tablespoons chopped canned *green chili peppers,* drained; and ⅛ teaspoon *garlic salt.* Cover and chill for up to 24 hours. Makes about ¾ cup.

Nutrition information per serving: 398 calories, 22 g protein, 49 g carbohydrate, 17 g fat (6 g saturated), 38 mg cholesterol, 801 mg sodium, 1,061 mg potassium.

BEEF AND THREE-CHEESE TORTELLINI SALAD

Cheese-filled pasta, cubes of Colby or cheddar, and grated Parmesan make up the trio of cheeses in this hearty make-ahead salad.

2 cups frozen *or* refrigerated cheese-filled tortellini (about 7 ounces)
8 ounces cooked lean beef *or* fully cooked lean ham, cut into thin strips (1½ cups)
1 cup cubed Colby *or* cheddar cheese (4 ounces)
1 cup broccoli flowerets
1 small yellow summer squash *or* zucchini, halved lengthwise and sliced (1 cup)
   Creamy Parmesan Dressing
   Curly endive *or* leaf lettuce
1 cup cherry tomatoes, halved

Cook tortellini according to package directions. Drain tortellini. Rinse with cold water; drain again.

In a large mixing bowl combine tortellini, beef or ham strips, Colby or cheddar cheese, broccoli flowerets, and sliced yellow summer squash. Pour Creamy Parmesan Dressing over beef mixture. Toss lightly to coat. Cover and chill for 4 to 24 hours.

To serve, line four salad plates with curly endive or leaf lettuce. Divide beef mixture among plates. Garnish each serving with cherry tomatoes. Makes 4 servings.

Creamy Parmesan Dressing: In a small mixing bowl combine ½ cup *mayonnaise or salad dressing,* 2 tablespoons grated *Parmesan cheese,* 1 tablespoon snipped fresh or 1 teaspoon crushed dried *marjoram,* 1 tablespoon *red wine vinegar,* and ¼ teaspoon *pepper.*

Nutrition information per serving: 593 calories, 31 g protein, 32 g carbohydrate, 39 g fat (11 g saturated), 111 mg cholesterol, 641 mg sodium, 551 mg potassium.

WARM BEEF SALAD WITH BLUE CHEESE

Use roast beef from the local deli in this tasty salad.

1   cup sliced fresh mushrooms
½   cup thinly sliced celery
2   small tomatoes, seeded and chopped
¼   cup chopped green pepper
3   tablespoons olive oil *or* cooking oil
¼   cup red wine vinegar
½   cup sliced red onion
1   teaspoon Worcestershire sauce
1   teaspoon snipped fresh basil *or*
       ½ teaspoon dried basil, crushed
1   teaspoon snipped fresh oregano *or*
       ½ teaspoon dried oregano, crushed
¼   teaspoon salt
¼   teaspoon pepper
6   ounces cooked lean beef, cut into bite-
       size strips
⅔   cup canned garbanzo beans, rinsed
       and drained
    Spinach leaves
2   tablespoons crumbled blue cheese

Combine mushrooms, celery, tomatoes, and green pepper; set aside.

In a skillet heat *2 tablespoons* of the oil and *2 tablespoons* of the vinegar. Add onion; cover and cook for 2 minutes. Remove onion with a slotted spoon; add to mushroom mixture. Add the remaining oil and vinegar, Worcestershire sauce, basil, oregano, salt, and pepper to skillet. Stir in beef and garbanzo beans. Heat through. Add mushroom mixture. Toss to mix.

Divide beef mixture among three spinach-lined salad plates. Sprinkle with blue cheese. Makes 3 servings.

Nutrition information per serving: 386 calories, 25 g protein, 27 g carbohydrate, 21 g fat (5 g saturated), 59 mg cholesterol, 323 mg sodium, 902 mg potassium.

PACIFIC RIM GRILLED PORK SALAD

*This dazzling salad blends grilled pork with ingredients from the eastern rim of the Pacific Ocean—
soy sauce, ginger, hoisin sauce, rice wine vinegar, sesame oil, and enoki mushrooms.*

⅓ cup water
¼ cup dry sherry
¼ cup soy sauce
4 teaspoons grated gingerroot
3 cloves garlic, minced
1 1½-pound boneless pork loin roast,
      cut into ½-inch-thick slices
¼ cup hoisin sauce
2 tablespoons brown sugar
2 tablespoons salad oil
2 tablespoons rice wine vinegar *or* white
      wine vinegar
1 tablespoon toasted sesame oil
12 cups torn spinach
6 thin red onion slices, separated
      into rings
1 tablespoon sesame seed, toasted
      (optional)
1 pound plums, pitted and sliced
      (3 cups)
    Enoki mushrooms (optional)

For marinade, in a small mixing bowl combine water, sherry, soy sauce, gingerroot, and garlic. Reserve *2 tablespoons* of the marinade for the dressing. Place meat in a plastic bag set in a large bowl. Pour remaining marinade over meat. Close bag. Refrigerate for 1 hour.

Drain meat, discarding marinade. Grill meat, uncovered, directly over medium-hot coals for 10 to 12 minutes or till just a little pink remains in the center, turning once.

Meanwhile, for dressing, in a saucepan combine the reserved 2 tablespoons marinade, hoisin sauce, brown sugar, salad oil, and vinegar. Bring to boiling. Stir in sesame oil. Remove from heat.

Thinly slice meat into bite-size strips. In a large salad bowl combine meat, spinach, onion slices, and, if desired, sesame seed. Pour hot dressing over meat mixture. Toss gently to coat.

Serve on salad plates with plum slices. Top with enoki mushrooms, if desired. Makes 6 servings.

Nutrition information per serving: 310 calories, 21 g protein, 22 g carbohydrate, 16 g fat (4 g saturated), 51 mg cholesterol, 1,159 mg sodium, 1,047 mg potassium.

ASIAN PORK-CABBAGE SALAD

Rice vinegars, used frequently in Oriental cooking, are made from rice wine or sake and are usually clear to pale gold in color. They have a subtle tang and slightly sweet flavor.

1 3-ounce package pork-flavored ramen
   noodles
¼ cup rice vinegar *or* white wine vinegar
2 tablespoons salad oil
1 tablespoon sugar
½ teaspoon toasted sesame oil
¼ teaspoon pepper
1 8¾-ounce can baby corn, drained
1 cup fresh pea pods *or* ½ of a 6-ounce
   package frozen pea pods, thawed
2 cups shredded cabbage
8 ounces cooked lean pork, cut into
   bite-size strips (1½ cups)
½ of a 14-ounce can straw mushrooms
   (1 cup) *or* one 6-ounce can whole
   mushrooms, drained
¼ cup sliced green onions
¼ cup sliced radishes
   Bok choy leaves
2 teaspoons sesame seed, toasted

Cook ramen noodles according to package directions, omitting the seasoning package. Drain and set aside.

Meanwhile, for dressing, in a screw-top jar combine the seasoning package from the ramen noodles, vinegar, salad oil, sugar, sesame oil, and pepper. Cover and shake well to dissolve seasonings.

Cut each ear of baby corn in half crosswise. If using fresh pea pods, trim ends and remove strings. In a large mixing bowl combine cooked noodles, baby corn, pea pods, cabbage, pork, mushrooms, green onions, and radishes. Shake dressing well. Pour over cabbage mixture. Toss lightly to coat. Cover and chill for 4 to 24 hours.

Line four salad plates with bok choy leaves. Divide pork mixture among the plates. Sprinkle each with sesame seed. Makes 4 servings.

Nutrition information per serving: 386 calories, 23 g protein, 31 g carbohydrate, 20 g fat (4 g saturated), 52 mg cholesterol, 830 mg sodium, 870 mg potassium.

SOUTHWESTERN-STYLE PORK AND BLACK BEAN SALAD

Serve this colorful, chili-flavored salad with an ice-cold pitcher of lemonade or limeade.

1   15-ounce can black beans, rinsed and drained
8   ounces cooked lean pork, cut into bite-size strips (1½ cups)
1   8-ounce can red kidney beans, rinsed and drained
1   8-ounce can whole kernel corn, drained
½   cup chopped green pepper
¼   cup chopped red onion
¼   cup salad oil
¼   cup vinegar
2   tablespoons snipped fresh cilantro
2   tablespoons lime juice
1   tablespoon sugar
1   teaspoon chili powder
1   teaspoon ground cumin
¼   teaspoon salt
1   clove garlic, minced
    Shredded leaf lettuce
    Tortilla chips (optional)

In a large mixing bowl combine black beans, pork, kidney beans, corn, green pepper, and onion.

For dressing, in a screw-top jar combine oil, vinegar, cilantro, lime juice, sugar, chili powder, cumin, salt, and garlic. Cover and shake well. Pour dressing over pork mixture. Toss lightly to coat. Cover and chill for 4 to 24 hours, stirring occasionally.

To serve, line six salad plates with leaf lettuce. Divide the pork mixture among the lettuce-lined plates. Serve with tortilla chips, if desired. Makes 6 servings.

Nutrition information per serving: 303 calories, 19 g protein, 28 g carbohydrate, 16 g fat (3 g saturated), 36 mg cholesterol, 450 mg sodium, 647 mg potassium.

HAM AND FRUIT TOSSED SALAD

Watching fat and cholesterol? Use turkey ham in this one-dish meal.

2   medium oranges
1   3-ounce package cream cheese,
         softened
2   teaspoons sugar
¼   cup orange juice
3   cups torn iceberg lettuce
3   cups torn spinach
8   ounces cubed fully cooked ham
         (1½ cups)
1   cup red *or* green seedless grapes,
         halved
¼   cup Spicy Nuts (see recipe, page 140)
     Orange peel (optional)

Finely shred enough peel from *1* of the oranges to equal *1 teaspoon;* set orange peel aside. Peel and slice the oranges crosswise. Cut each slice in half. Set orange slices aside.

For dressing, in a small mixing bowl beat together cream cheese, sugar, and the reserved orange peel till smooth. Gradually beat in enough of the orange juice to make dressing of drizzling consistency. Set dressing aside.

In a large mixing bowl combine lettuce, spinach, ham, grapes, Spicy Nuts, and orange slices. Toss lightly to mix. Pour dressing over lettuce mixture. Toss lightly to coat. Divide among four salad plates. Garnish with additional orange peel, if desired. Makes 4 servings.

Nutrition information per serving: 286 calories, 17 g protein, 20 g carbohydrate, 17 g fat (6 g saturated), 53 mg cholesterol, 808 mg sodium, 686 mg potassium.

MINTED HAM SALAD

When you need supper on the table double-quick, chill this salad in the freezer for 20 minutes.

1   8-ounce carton plain yogurt
1   tablespoon milk
2   teaspoons horseradish mustard
1   tablespoon snipped fresh mint *or* basil
        or 1 teaspoon dried mint *or* basil,
        crushed
⅛   teaspoon onion powder
3   cups broccoli flowerets, chopped
        sweet red pepper, cauliflower
        flowerets, *and/or* sliced zucchini
1   pound fully cooked ham, cut into
        ½-inch cubes
½   cup shredded cheddar cheese
        (2 ounces)
     Leaf lettuce

For dressing, combine yogurt, milk, mustard, mint or basil, and onion powder; set aside.

In a large mixing bowl combine vegetables, ham, and shredded cheese. Pour dressing over vegetable mixture; toss lightly to coat. Cover and chill for 4 to 24 hours.

To serve, line four salad plates with leaf lettuce. Divide vegetable mixture between the lettuce-lined salad plates. Makes 4 servings.

Nutrition information per serving: 265 calories, 33 g protein, 9 g carbohydrate, 11 g fat (5 g saturated), 50 mg cholesterol, 1,459 mg sodium, 800 mg potassium.

GERMAN-STYLE POTATO AND SAUSAGE SALAD

The addition of Polish sausage transforms this classic side-dish salad into a hearty main dish.

1½ pounds small red potatoes, cut into bite-size pieces

1 pound fully cooked Polish sausage *or* bratwurst, sliced

¾ cup chopped red *or* yellow sweet pepper

½ cup chopped onion

1 clove garlic, minced

1 tablespoon all-purpose flour

1 tablespoon sugar

1 tablespoon coarse-grain brown mustard

⅛ teaspoon pepper

½ cup chicken broth *or* water

¼ cup vinegar

¼ cup pickled banana pepper slices (optional)

In a covered saucepan cook potatoes in lightly salted boiling water about 10 minutes or till just tender. Drain well.

Meanwhile, in a large skillet cook Polish sausage or bratwurst for 2 to 3 minutes or till lightly browned. Remove sausage from skillet, reserving drippings in skillet. Drain sausage on paper towels.

For dressing, cook sweet pepper, onion, and garlic in reserved drippings till tender but not brown. Stir in flour, sugar, mustard, and pepper. Stir in chicken broth or water and vinegar.

Cook and stir till thickened and bubbly. Stir in cooked potatoes, sausage, and, if desired, banana pepper slices. Cook for 2 to 3 minutes more or till heated through, stirring gently. Serve immediately. Makes 4 servings.

Nutrition information per serving: 584 calories, 21 g protein, 48 g carbohydrate, 37 g fat (11 g saturated), 76 mg cholesterol, 1,199 mg sodium, 1,155 mg potassium.

ROASTED PEPPER-PEPPERONI SALAD

Roasting the sweet peppers gives them a more mellow flavor. If you can't find an assortment of colored sweet peppers, use all green peppers.

2   large green sweet peppers
2   large red *or* purple sweet peppers
2   large yellow *or* orange sweet peppers
½   of a 15-ounce can garbanzo beans, rinsed and drained (¾ cup)
4   ounces Monterey Jack cheese, cut into strips
¼   cup olive oil *or* salad oil
¼   cup red wine vinegar
2   cloves garlic, minced
½   teaspoon dry mustard
¼   teaspoon salt
⅛   teaspoon pepper
6   cups torn curly endive *and/or* Belgian endive leaves
1   3½- to 4-ounce package sliced pepperoni
    Greek olives (optional)

To roast peppers, halve all of the sweet peppers. Remove stems, seeds, and membranes. Place peppers, cut side down, on a foil-lined baking sheet. Bake in a 425° oven for 20 to 25 minutes or till skin is bubbly and browned. Place peppers in a new brown paper bag. Seal and let stand for 20 to 30 minutes or till cool enough to handle. Peel skin from peppers. Cut peppers lengthwise into ½-inch-wide strips.

In a large bowl combine pepper strips, garbanzo beans, and cheese strips. In a screw-top jar combine oil, vinegar, garlic, mustard, salt, and pepper. Cover; shake well. Pour over roasted pepper mixture; toss lightly till coated.

Arrange curly endive and/or Belgian endive leaves on four salad plates. Divide the pepper mixture among the plates. Add pepperoni to plates. Garnish with Greek olives, if desired. Makes 4 servings.

Nutrition information per serving: 466 calories, 17 g protein, 25 g carbohydrate, 34 g fat (12 g saturated), 45 mg cholesterol, 961 mg sodium, 614 mg potassium.

GREEK SALAD WITH HERBED VINAIGRETTE

No leftover lamb around? Broil some lamb chops to medium-rare. Then, chill the chops completely before slicing them into thin strips.

3   cups torn curly endive *or* romaine
½   cups torn iceberg lettuce *or* spinach
6   ounces cooked lean lamb, pork, *or* beef, cut into bite-size strips
1   medium tomato, chopped
½   small cucumber, thinly sliced
6   radishes, sliced
2   tablespoons sliced pitted ripe olives
½   cup crumbled feta cheese (2 ounces)
2   green onions, thinly sliced
½   cup Herbed Vinaigrette
3   anchovy fillets, drained, rinsed, and patted dry (optional)

Toss together curly endive or romaine and lettuce or spinach. Divide greens among three salad plates.

Arrange meat strips, chopped tomato, sliced cucumber, sliced radishes, and olives on greens. Sprinkle with feta cheese and green onions. Shake Herbed Vinaigrette well. Drizzle over salads. Top with anchovy fillets, if desired. Makes 3 servings.

Herbed Vinaigrette: In a screw-top jar combine ½ cup *salad oil;* ⅓ cup *white wine vinegar or vinegar;* 1 tablespoon *sugar;* 2 teaspoons snipped fresh or ½ teaspoon crushed, dried *thyme, oregano, or basil;* ½ teaspoon *paprika;* ¼ teaspoon *dry mustard;* and ⅛ teaspoon *pepper.* Cover and shake well. Store any remaining dressing in the refrigerator for up to 2 weeks. Shake well before using. Makes about ¾ cup.

Nutrition information per serving: 431 calories, 20 g protein, 11 g carbohydrate, 35 g fat (8 g saturated), 69 mg cholesterol, 325 mg sodium, 627 mg potassium.

LAMB-PASTA SALAD WITH APRICOT DRESSING

Put any leftover lamb or beef to delicious use in this colorful salad.

1⅓ cups corkscrew macaroni

8 ounces cooked lean lamb *or* beef, cut into bite-size strips (1½ cups)

1 small zucchini, halved lengthwise and sliced (1 cup)

1 medium red sweet pepper, cut into thin, bite-size strips (1 cup)

½ cup snipped dried apricots

¼ cup raisins

Apricot Dressing

Boston *or* Bibb lettuce leaves

Milk

Parsley sprigs (optional)

Cook pasta according to package directions. Drain pasta. Rinse with cold water; drain again.

In a large mixing bowl combine pasta, lamb or beef, zucchini, sweet pepper, apricots, and raisins. Pour Apricot Dressing over pasta mixture. Toss lightly to coat. Cover and chill for 4 to 24 hours.

To serve, line four salad plates with Boston or Bibb lettuce leaves. If necessary, stir a little milk (1 to 2 tablespoons) into the pasta mixture to moisten. Divide pasta mixture among lettuce-lined plates. Garnish with parsley sprigs, if desired. Makes 4 servings.

Apricot Dressing: In a small mixing bowl stir together ⅔ cup *plain yogurt,* 2 tablespoons *apricot preserves,* 1 tablespoon snipped fresh *parsley,* ¼ teaspoon *salt,* and ⅛ teaspoon *pepper.*

Nutrition information per serving: 556 calories, 14 g protein, 48 g carbohydrate, 35 g fat (16 g saturated), 67 mg cholesterol, 217 mg sodium, 723 mg potassium.

COUSCOUS-LAMB SALAD

Couscous is a small, hard grain product from North Africa that gets soft and fluffy when it's added to boiling water. Look for couscous in the rice or pasta section of your supermarket.

1　cup chicken broth
½　cup couscous
¼　cup olive oil *or* salad oil
3　tablespoons vinegar
2　tablespoons dry red wine
1　tablespoon sugar
1　teaspoon snipped fresh thyme *or*
　　¼ teaspoon dried thyme, crushed
1　teaspoon snipped fresh oregano *or*
　　¼ teaspoon dried oregano, crushed
¼　teaspoon ground cumin
⅛　teaspoon pepper
1　clove garlic, minced
8　ounces cooked lean lamb *or* pork,
　　cut into bite-size strips (1½ cups)
½　medium cucumber, seeded and
　　chopped (1 cup)
½　of a 15-ounce can garbanzo beans,
　　rinsed and drained (¾ cup)
½　cup shredded carrot
½　cup sliced radishes
3　tablespoons sliced green onions
　　Purple salad savoy leaves

In a small saucepan bring chicken broth to boiling. Remove from heat. Stir in couscous. Cover and let stand for 5 minutes or till liquid is absorbed.

Meanwhile, for dressing, in a screw-top jar combine oil, vinegar, red wine, sugar, thyme, oregano, cumin, pepper, and garlic. Cover and shake well. Set dressing aside.

In a large mixing bowl combine couscous, lamb or pork, cucumber, garbanzo beans, carrot, radishes, and green onions. Shake dressing well; pour over salad mixture. Toss lightly to coat. Cover and chill for 4 to 6 hours. Serve on salad plates lined with salad savoy leaves. Makes 4 servings.

Nutrition information per serving: 414 calories, 23 g protein, 34 g carbohydrate, 20 g fat (4 g saturated), 52 mg cholesterol, 430 mg sodium, 573 mg potassium.

CHICKEN AND RASPBERRY SPINACH SALAD

Vary the fruit in this luscious main-dish salad by adding blueberries or strawberries instead of raspberries.

¼ cup raspberry vinegar *or* white wine
     vinegar
2 tablespoons salad oil
1 tablespoon honey
½ teaspoon finely shredded orange peel
¼ teaspoon pepper
⅛ teaspoon salt
4 skinless, boneless medium chicken
     breast halves (about 12 ounces
     total)
2 tablespoons cooking oil
8 to 10 cups torn spinach *or* torn mixed
     greens
1 cup fresh raspberries
1 papaya, peeled, seeded, and sliced;
     2 medium nectarines, pitted and
     sliced; *or* 2 peaches, peeled, pitted
     and sliced

For dressing, in a screw-top jar combine vinegar, oil, honey, orange peel, pepper, and salt. Cover and shake well. Chill dressing till serving time.

In a medium skillet cook chicken in hot oil over medium heat for 8 to 10 minutes or till chicken is tender and no longer pink, turning often to brown evenly. Remove chicken from skillet. Cut into thin, bite-size strips.

In a large bowl toss together warm chicken strips and spinach or mixed greens. Shake dressing well. Add dressing and raspberries to the chicken mixture. Toss lightly to coat well. Divide the chicken mixture among four salad plates. Arrange papaya, nectarine, or peach slices on each plate. Makes 4 servings.

Nutrition information per serving: 329 calories, 20 g protein, 28 g carbohydrate, 17 g fat (3 g saturated), 45 mg cholesterol, 203 mg sodium, 1,027 mg potassium.

GRILLED CHICKEN SALAD WITH PLUM VINAIGRETTE

For a rainbow of color, use several plum varieties—Kelsey with yellow skin and meat, Queen Ann with purple skin and golden meat, Red Beaut with red skin and yellow meat, Santa Rosa with crimson skin and yellow meat, or Ace with red skin and red meat.

⅓ cup white wine vinegar

¼ cup bottled plum sauce, plum preserves, *or* sweet-and-sour sauce

3 tablespoons salad oil

¼ teaspoon ground coriander

¼ teaspoon coarsely cracked pepper

1 pound skinless, boneless chicken breast halves, cut into 2x1-inch strips

4 medium plums

1 cup fresh pea pods *or* ½ of a 6-ounce package frozen pea pods, thawed

6 cups torn mixed greens

For plum vinaigrette, in a screw-top jar combine vinegar, plum sauce, salad oil, coriander, and pepper. Cover and shake well. Reserve *¼ cup* of the vinaigrette for brushing sauce. Set aside remaining vinaigrette for the salad dressing.

Soak sixteen 5- to 6-inch long wooden skewers in hot water for 5 minutes. Thread chicken strips, accordion-style, onto *8* of the skewers. Cut each plum into 8 wedges. Thread plum wedges onto the remaining skewers.

Grill chicken directly over medium-hot coals for 8 to 10 minutes or till chicken is tender and no longer pink, adding the skewered plums during the last 3 minutes and brushing chicken and plums occasionally with the reserved plum vinaigrette.

Meanwhile, if using fresh pea pods, trim ends and remove strings. In a large bowl toss together the pea pods and mixed greens. Divide greens mixture among four salad plates. Arrange chicken and plum skewers atop greens mixture. Shake remaining plum vinaigrette well. Drizzle plum vinaigrette over each serving. Makes 4 servings.

Nutrition information per serving: 304 calories, 26 g protein, 20 g carbohydrate, 15 g fat (2 g saturated), 59 mg cholesterol, 73 mg sodium, 585 mg potassium.

CHICKEN SALAD WITH TAHINI SAUCE

Tahini (tuh HEE nee) is a thick paste made of ground sesame seed. Look for it in the foreign foods section of your grocery store or in an Asian market.

4   skinless, boneless medium chicken breast halves (about 12 ounces)
6   to 10 green onions, cut into thin, bite-size strips
2   small carrots, cut into thin, bite-size strips
¼   cup tahini (sesame paste)
3   tablespoons soy sauce
3   tablespoons red wine vinegar
2   tablespoons salad oil
2   teaspoons sugar
½   to 1 teaspoon chili oil *or* ½ to 1 teaspoon crushed red pepper
1   clove garlic, minced
1   to 2 tablespoons brewed tea, cooled, *or* water (optional)
4   to 6 cups shredded bok choy, romaine, *or* Chinese cabbage
2   to 3 tablespoons peanuts

Place chicken on the unheated rack of a broiler pan. Broil 4 to 5 inches from the heat for 12 to 15 minutes or till tender and no longer pink, turning once. Cut chicken into thin, bite-size strips.

In a large mixing bowl combine cooked chicken strips, green onions, and carrots. Cover and chill till serving time.

For tahini sauce, stir together the tahini, soy sauce, vinegar, salad oil, sugar, chili oil or crushed red pepper, and garlic. If necessary, thin sauce with a little brewed tea or water.

To serve, divide shredded greens among four salad plates. Place chicken mixture atop greens. Drizzle with tahini sauce. Sprinkle with peanuts. Makes 4 servings.

Nutrition information per serving: 308 calories, 22 g protein, 14 g carbohydrate, 20 g fat (3 g saturated), 45 mg cholesterol, 842 mg sodium, 523 mg potassium.

GRILLED CALIFORNIA CHICKEN SALAD

For a variation, try this salad with yellow wax beans instead of green beans and sliced carambola (star fruit) instead of the mango.

Cilantro Vinaigrette
2 skinless, boneless chicken breast
   halves (about 8 ounces)
1 cup green beans
4 cups shredded mixed greens
1 orange, sliced
1 mango, seeded, peeled, and sliced
   Chopped peanuts *or* toasted sesame
   seed (optional)

Prepare Cilantro Vinaigrette. Reserve *half* of the vinaigrette for dressing. Rinse chicken; pat dry. In a medium bowl combine remaining vinaigrette and chicken. Cover; marinate in the refrigerator for 30 minutes. Drain, reserving marinade.

Grill chicken on an uncovered grill directly over medium-high coals for 15 to 18 minutes or till tender and no longer pink, turning once and brushing with reserved marinade during the last 5 minutes of grilling. Discard any remaining marinade.

Meanwhile, in a small saucepan cook the green beans, uncovered, in a small amount of boiling water about 15 minutes or till crisp-tender. Drain beans.

To serve, divide shredded greens between two salad plates. Slice each chicken breast crosswise into 6 to 8 pieces. Reassemble chicken breasts on greens. Arrange cooked beans, orange slices, and mango slices on greens. Shake reserved vinaigrette well. Drizzle vinaigrette over each serving. Sprinkle with chopped peanuts or sesame seed, if desired. Makes 2 servings.

Cilantro Vinaigrette: In a screw-top jar combine ¼ cup *papaya or apricot nectar,* 3 tablespoons snipped fresh *cilantro,* 2 tablespoons *olive oil or salad oil,* 2 tablespoons *rice wine vinegar or white wine vinegar,* 1 teaspoon *toasted sesame oil,* ½ teaspoon *ground ginger,* and ⅛ to ¼ teaspoon *ground red pepper.* Cover and shake well. Store in refrigerator for up to 2 weeks. Shake well before serving. Makes ½ cup.

Nutrition information per serving: 427 calories, 25 g protein, 37 g carbohydrate, 22 g fat (4 g saturated), 59 mg cholesterol, 78 mg sodium, 855 mg potassium.

SANTE FE CHICKEN SALAD

If you would rather, broil the chicken breasts 4 inches from the heat for 6 to 8 minutes, turning once.

4 skinless, boneless medium chicken breast halves (about 12 ounces total)
¼ cup salad oil
2 tablespoons white wine vinegar *or* white vinegar
2 tablespoons lime juice
½ teaspoon chili powder
¼ teaspoon dry mustard
5 to 6 drops bottled hot pepper sauce
1 15-ounce can black beans, rinsed and drained
1 8¾-ounce can whole kernel corn, drained
1 large red *or* yellow sweet pepper, cut into thin, bite-size strips (1¼ cups)
  Green salad savoy leaves
1 large avocado, seeded, peeled, and cut into bite-size pieces
½ cup finely shredded Monterey Jack *or* cheddar cheese (2 ounces)
  Fresh Salsa

Rinse chicken; pat dry. Place chicken in a plastic bag set in a deep bowl. For marinade, in a screw-top jar combine salad oil, vinegar, lime juice, chili powder, dry mustard, and bottled hot pepper sauce. Cover; shake well. Pour *¼ cup* of the marinade over chicken. Close bag; turn to coat. Marinate in the refrigerator for 2 hours, turning bag occasionally.

Meanwhile, place black beans in a bowl. In another bowl mix corn and sweet pepper. Divide remaining marinade between the 2 bowls. Cover; marinate at room temperature for 2 hours, stirring often.

Drain chicken. Discard marinade. Grill chicken on an uncovered grill directly over medium-hot coals for 15 to 18 minutes or till tender and no longer pink. Turn chicken halfway through grilling time.

Line four salad plates with salad savoy leaves. Cut the chicken breast halves crosswise into slices. Reassemble on greens. Divide black beans, corn mixture, avocado, and cheese among the salad plates.

Pour some of the Fresh Salsa over each chicken breast. Pass remaining Fresh Salsa. Makes 4 servings.

Fresh Salsa: In a medium mixing bowl stir together 1½ cups finely chopped, peeled *tomatoes;* ¼ cup sliced *green onions;* 2 tablespoons chopped *green pepper;* 2 tablespoons snipped fresh *cilantro or parsley;* 2 tablespoons *lemon juice;* 1 *jalapeño pepper,* cut up (not seeded); 1 clove *garlic,* minced; and ⅛ teaspoon *pepper.* Place *half* of the mixture in a blender container or food processor bowl. Cover and blend or process till finely chopped. Return all of the salsa mixture to mixing bowl. Cover and chill for several hours or overnight, stirring occasionally. Bring to room temperature before serving. Makes 2 cups.

Nutrition information per serving: 477 calories, 31 g protein, 41 g carbohydrate, 26 g fat (5 g saturated), 57 mg cholesterol, 541 mg sodium, 1,286 mg potassium.

SWEET-AND-SOUR STIR-FRY CHICKEN SALAD

Simplify this easy-to-fix recipe even more by using 1 cup of bottled sweet-and-sour sauce instead of making your own.

4 skinless, boneless medium chicken breast halves (about 12 ounces total)
8 cups mesclun *or* 6 cups torn romaine and 2 cups torn escarole
1 tablespoon salad oil
1 cup thinly bias-sliced carrots
1 medium red sweet pepper, cut into ¾-inch pieces (1 cup)
4 green onions, bias-sliced into 1-inch pieces
  Sweet-and-Sour Sauce
1 8-ounce can pineapple tidbits (juice pack), drained

Rinse chicken; pat dry. Cut chicken into bite-size strips; set aside. Divide greens among four salad plates; set aside.

Pour oil into a wok or large skillet. (Add more oil as necessary during cooking.) Preheat over medium-high heat. Add carrots to wok; stir-fry for 2 minutes. Add red sweet pepper and green onions to wok; stir-fry for 2 to 3 minutes more or till vegetables are crisp-tender. Remove vegetables from wok.

Add chicken to wok or skillet; stir-fry for 2 to 3 minutes or till no longer pink. Push chicken from the center of the wok. Stir Sweet-and-Sour Sauce; add to center of wok. Cook and stir till thickened and bubbly. Cook and stir for 2 minutes more.

Return vegetables to wok. Add pineapple. Stir all ingredients together to coat with sauce. Spoon hot chicken mixture on each plate of greens. Makes 4 servings.

Sweet-and-Sour Sauce: In a small mixing bowl combine ½ cup packed *brown sugar* and 1 tablespoon *cornstarch*. Stir in ⅓ cup *chicken broth;* ⅓ cup *red wine vinegar;* 1 tablespoon *soy sauce;* 1 teaspoon grated *gingerroot;* and 1 clove *garlic,* minced.

Nutrition information per serving: 331 calories, 21 g protein, 51 g carbohydrate, 6 g fat (1 g saturated), 45 mg cholesterol, 429 mg sodium, 1,105 mg potassium.

GARLIC-GINGER CHICKEN STRIP SALAD

If you're watching your sodium, switch to reduced-sodium soy sauce.

4 skinless, boneless medium chicken
   breast halves (about 12 ounces
   total)
¼ cup soy sauce
¼ cup dry sherry
1 tablespoon snipped fresh basil *or*
   1 teaspoon dried basil, crushed
1 tablespoon honey
2 teaspoons grated gingerroot
½ teaspoon crushed red pepper
½ teaspoon ground black pepper
¼ teaspoon five-spice powder
4 cloves garlic, minced
2 cups broccoli flowerets
5 cups torn mixed greens
1 cup enoki mushrooms *or* sliced fresh
   mushrooms
1 medium red sweet pepper, cut into
   ¾-inch pieces (1 cup)
1 cup coarsely chopped red cabbage
   Leaf lettuce
   Oriental Salad Dressing

Cut each chicken breast half into bite-size strips. For marinade, in a medium mixing bowl combine soy sauce, sherry, basil, honey, gingerroot, red pepper, black pepper, five-spice powder, and garlic. Add chicken strips; stir to coat. Cover and refrigerate for 4 to 24 hours.

Drain chicken strips, reserving marinade. Place chicken strips on the unheated rack of a broiler pan. Broil 4 to 5 inches from heat about 5 minutes or till light brown, brushing once with reserved marinade. Turn and brush again. Broil 3 to 5 minutes more or till chicken is golden brown and no longer pink. Discard remaining marinade.`

Meanwhile, in a medium saucepan cook broccoli, covered, in a small amount of boiling water for 1 minute. Drain well and chill.

In a large mixing bowl toss together torn mixed greens, mushrooms, red sweet pepper, red cabbage, and cooked broccoli. Shake Oriental Salad Dressing well. Pour about ½ *cup* of the dressing over greens mixture; toss lightly to coat. Line four salad plates with leaf lettuce. Divide greens mixture among salad plates. Top with chicken strips. Pour remaining dressing over chicken. Makes 4 servings.

Oriental Salad Dressing: In a screw-top jar combine ⅓ cup *unsweetened pineapple juice*, ¼ cup *rice vinegar or white vinegar*, 1 tablespoon *soy sauce*, 2 teaspoons *sugar*, 1½ teaspoons *toasted sesame oil*, and ¼ teaspoon *ground black pepper*. Cover and shake well. Makes about ⅔ cup.

Nutrition information per serving: 235 calories, 21 g protein, 26 g carbohydrate, 5 g fat (1 g saturated), 45 mg cholesterol, 1,368 mg sodium, 881 mg potassium.

CHICKEN AND FRUIT PLATES WITH HONEY-JALAPEÑO DRESSING

Use a spatula to transfer the sliced chicken breast halves from your cutting board to the salad plates.

4   skinless, boneless medium chicken breast halves (about 12 ounces total)
½   teaspoon lemon-pepper seasoning
1   tablespoon cooking oil
6   cups torn mixed greens
3   cups strawberries, halved
1   15¼-ounce can pineapple spears, drained
1   medium avocado, seeded, peeled, and sliced
½   cup alfalfa sprouts
    Honey-Jalapeño Dressing

Sprinkle both sides of chicken breasts with lemon-pepper seasoning. In a large skillet cook chicken in hot oil over medium-high heat for 5 to 6 minutes per side or till golden brown and no longer pink. Remove chicken from skillet. Cut diagonally into ½-inch-wide strips.

Meanwhile, divide mixed greens among four salad plates. Reassemble chicken breast halves atop greens. Arrange strawberry halves, pineapple spears, avocado slices, and alfalfa sprouts on each plate. Pour Honey-Jalapeño Dressing over salads. Makes 4 servings.

Honey-Jalapeño Dressing: In a blender container or food processor bowl combine ½ cup *mayonnaise or salad dressing;* 2 tablespoons *honey;* 1 tablespoon *lime juice or lemon juice;* 1 tablespoon *coarse-grain brown mustard;* 1 *jalapeño pepper,* cut up (not seeded); and ¼ teaspoon *paprika.* Cover and blend or process till dressing is smooth. Makes about ⅔ cup.

Nutrition information per serving: 527 calories, 21 g protein, 33 g carbohydrate, 37 g fat (5 g saturated), 61 mg cholesterol, 418 mg sodium, 1,062 mg potassium.

CHICKEN FAJITA SALAD

The Tortilla Cups can be made up to five days ahead. Just store them in an airtight container.

4 skinless, boneless medium chicken breast halves (about 12 ounces total)
½ cup Italian salad dressing
½ cup salsa
1 tablespoon salad oil
1 small yellow summer squash *or* zucchini, cut into thin, bite-size strips (1 cup)
1 medium red sweet pepper, cut into thin, bite-size strips (1 cup)
3 green onions, bias-sliced into 1-inch pieces (⅓ cup)
4 Tortilla Cups (see recipe, page 17)
Dairy sour cream (optional)
Frozen avocado dip, thawed (optional)
Salsa (optional)
½ cup shredded cheddar cheese (2 ounces)
4 cups shredded iceberg lettuce
1 cup chopped tomato

Rinse chicken; pat dry. Cut chicken into bite-size strips; set aside.

For marinade, in a large mixing bowl combine Italian salad dressing and the ½ cup salsa. Add chicken strips to marinade; stir to coat. Cover and refrigerate for 4 to 24 hours. Drain chicken strips, discarding the marinade.

Pour oil into a large skillet. (Add more oil as necessary during cooking.) Preheat over medium-high heat. Add summer squash or zucchini; cook and stir about 2 minutes or till crisp-tender. Remove from skillet. Add sweet pepper and green onions to skillet; cook and stir for 2 to 3 minutes or till vegetables are crisp-tender. Remove from skillet. Add chicken to skillet; cook and stir for 2 to 3 minutes or till no longer pink.

To serve, place Tortilla Cups on salad plates. Divide chicken strips and vegetables among the Tortilla Cups. If desired, top each with sour cream, avocado dip, and salsa. Sprinkle with cheese. Arrange lettuce and tomato on plates alongside Tortilla Cups. Makes 4 servings.

Nutrition information per serving: 389 calories, 24 g protein, 23 g carbohydrate, 23 g fat (5 g saturated), 69 mg cholesterol, 488 mg sodium, 422 mg potassium.

PASTA CHICKEN SALAD

Cooking for two? Simply reduce the ingredients in this yummy salad by half.

1   cup tricolor *or* plain corkscrew
      macaroni
⅔ cup plain yogurt
¼ cup mayonnaise *or* salad dressing
2   tablespoons grated Parmesan cheese
½ teaspoon garlic salt
½ teaspoon dried Italian seasoning,
      crushed
    Dash pepper
2   cups coleslaw mix (shredded cabbage
      and carrot)
2   cups chopped cooked chicken
      (10 ounces)
1   medium tomato, seeded and chopped
    Leaf lettuce

Cook pasta according to package directions. Drain pasta. Rinse with cold water; drain again.

For dressing, in a large mixing bowl stir together yogurt, mayonnaise or salad dressing, Parmesan cheese, garlic salt, Italian seasoning, and pepper. Stir in pasta, coleslaw mix, and cooked chicken. Cover and chill for 4 to 24 hours.

Stir in tomato just before serving. Serve on lettuce-lined plates. Makes 4 servings.

Nutrition information per serving: 368 calories, 29 g protein, 22 g carbohydrate, 18 g fat (4 g saturated), 79 mg cholesterol, 502 mg sodium, 525 mg potassium.

CURRIED CHICKEN SALAD

To store this colorful, fruit and chicken salad longer than 8 hours, add the mandarin orange sections just before serving.

3   cups chopped cooked chicken
     (about 1 pound)
1¾ cups seedless red grapes, halved
1   11-ounce can mandarin orange
     sections, drained
1   8-ounce can sliced water chestnuts,
     drained
1   cup sliced celery
¾   cup mayonnaise *or* salad dressing
2   teaspoons soy sauce
2   teaspoons lemon juice
1   teaspoon curry powder
    Leaf lettuce

In a large mixing bowl combine chicken, grapes, mandarin orange sections, water chestnuts, and celery.

For dressing, in a small mixing bowl stir together mayonnaise or salad dressing, soy sauce, lemon juice, and curry powder. Mix well. Stir dressing into chicken mixture; toss lightly to coat. Cover and chill for up to 8 hours.

To serve, line salad plates with lettuce leaves. Top with chicken mixture. Makes 6 to 8 servings.

Nutrition information per serving: 418 calories, 24 g protein, 20 g carbohydrate, 28 g fat (5 g saturated), 84 mg cholesterol, 364 mg sodium, 421 mg potassium.

WALDORF TURKEY SALAD WITH CANTALOUPE

For a different look, serve this tasty salad on cantaloupe rings instead of wedges. Just cut the cantaloupe crosswise into four 1-inch-thick rings, then remove the seeds and rind.

1 cup vanilla yogurt
¼ teaspoon apple pie spice *or* pumpkin pie spice
   Dash salt
1 cup chopped pear *or* chopped apple
1 teaspoon lemon juice
2 cups chopped cooked turkey *or* chicken (10 ounces)
1 cup halved seedless red *or* green grapes
½ cup chopped celery
2 tablespoons sliced green onion
1 small cantaloupe
   Red-tip leaf lettuce
¼ cup slivered almonds, toasted

For dressing, in a small mixing bowl combine yogurt, apple pie spice or pumpkin pie spice, and salt. Set dressing aside.

In a medium mixing bowl toss pear or apple with lemon juice. Stir in turkey or chicken, grapes, celery, and green onion. Pour dressing over turkey mixture. Toss lightly to coat. Cover; chill for 2 to 24 hours.

To serve, cut cantaloupe into four wedges. Remove seeds and, if desired, the rind. Place cantaloupe wedges on lettuce-lined salad plates. Stir toasted almonds into turkey mixture. Spoon onto melon wedges. Makes 4 servings.

Nutrition information per serving: 359 calories, 27 g protein, 38 g carbohydrate, 12 g fat (3 g saturated), 75 mg cholesterol, 147 mg sodium, 976 mg potassium.

TOSSED CHICKEN SALAD WITH PEARS AND BLUE CHEESE

For variety, substitute apples for the pears. Or better yet, use one of each!

8   cups torn mixed greens
2½   cups cooked chicken *or* turkey cut
        into bite-size strips (about
        12 ounces)
2   medium pears, cored and sliced
1   large tomato, cut into wedges
¼   cup pear nectar
2   tablespoons walnut oil *or* salad oil
2   tablespoons white wine vinegar
1   tablespoon snipped fresh basil *or*
        1 teaspoon dried basil, crushed
¼   teaspoon dry mustard
⅛   teaspoon pepper
½   cup broken walnuts, toasted
⅓   cup crumbled blue cheese *or* feta
        cheese

In a large salad bowl combine torn mixed greens, chicken or turkey strips, pear slices, and tomato wedges. Toss lightly to mix.

For dressing, in a screw-top jar combine pear nectar, walnut oil or salad oil, vinegar, basil, mustard, and pepper. Cover and shake well. Pour dressing over salad. Toss lightly to coat.

Divide salad among four salad plates. Sprinkle each serving with walnuts and blue cheese or feta cheese. Makes 4 servings.

Nutrition information per serving: 460 calories, 35 g protein, 23 g carbohydrate, 27 g fat (6 g saturated), 93 mg cholesterol, 282 mg sodium, 900 mg potassium.

TARRAGON TURKEY SALAD WITH WILD RICE

Tarragon is a spicy, sharp-flavored herb with licoricelike overtones. It's often teamed with chicken or turkey.

⅓ cup wild rice
1 14½-ounce can chicken broth
⅓ cup long grain rice
2½ cups chopped cooked turkey *or* chicken (12 ounces)
½ cup bias-sliced celery
¼ cup sliced green onion
¼ cup olive oil *or* salad oil
2 tablespoons snipped fresh tarragon *or* 1 teaspoon dried tarragon, crushed
2 tablespoons white wine tarragon vinegar
2 tablespoons water
1 teaspoon Dijon-style mustard
¼ teaspoon salt
¼ teaspoon cracked black pepper
1 cup chopped apple
   Red-tip leaf lettuce
1 large apple, sliced (optional)

Rinse wild rice in a strainer under cold running water about 1 minute. In a medium saucepan combine wild rice and chicken broth. Bring to boiling; reduce heat. Cover and simmer for 20 minutes. Stir in the long grain rice. Return to boiling; reduce heat. Cover and simmer about 20 minutes more or till wild rice and long grain rice are tender and liquid is absorbed. Cool rice slightly (about 10 minutes).

In a large mixing bowl combine warm rice, turkey or chicken, celery, and green onion.

For dressing, in a screw-top jar combine oil, tarragon, vinegar, water, mustard, salt, and pepper. Cover and shake well. Pour dressing over rice mixture. Toss lightly to coat. Cover and chill for 2 to 24 hours.

To serve, stir chopped apple into the rice mixture. Line four salad plates with lettuce leaves. Divide the rice mixture among the salad plates. Garnish with apple slices, if desired. Makes 4 servings.

Nutrition information per serving: 443 calories, 33 g protein, 29 g carbohydrate, 22 g fat (4 g saturated) 85 mg cholesterol, 599 mg sodium, 527 mg potassium.

FRUITED CHICKEN-PASTA SALAD

Try any of the buttermilk ranch salad dressings—peppercorn, honey Dijon, or bacon—in this salad.

1   cup medium shell *or* elbow macaroni
1½ cups chopped cooked chicken *or* turkey (8 ounces)
1   11-ounce can mandarin orange sections, drained
1   cup seedless red *or* green grapes, halved
1   8-ounce can sliced water chestnuts, drained
½   cup sliced celery
½   cup buttermilk ranch salad dressing
⅛   teaspoon pepper
    Milk
    Leaf lettuce

Cook pasta according to package directions. Drain pasta. Rinse with cold water. Drain again.

In a large mixing bowl combine pasta, chicken or turkey, mandarin orange sections, grapes, water chestnuts, and celery.

For dressing, in a small mixing bowl combine buttermilk ranch dressing and pepper. Pour dressing over chicken mixture. Toss lightly to coat. Cover and chill for 4 to 24 hours.

Before serving, if necessary, stir in a little milk (1 to 2 tablespoons) to moisten. Serve on lettuce-lined salad plates. Makes 4 to 5 servings.

Nutrition information per serving: 387 calories, 16 g protein, 31 g carbohydrate, 22 g fat (4 g saturated), 37 mg cholesterol, 302 mg sodium, 369 mg potassium.

TURKEY SALAMI AND BEAN BOWL

Mustard and horseradish jazz up the dressing on this easy salad.

6   cups torn iceberg lettuce
1   small cucumber, halved lengthwise
      and thinly sliced (1½ cups)
1   8-ounce can red kidney beans, rinsed
      and drained
4   ounces turkey salami, cut into bite-
      size strips (about 1 cup)
1   cup thinly sliced carrot
¾   cup cubed provolone *or* Monterey
      Jack cheese (3 ounces)
2   tablespoons sliced green onion
⅓   cup mayonnaise *or* salad dressing
⅓   cup plain yogurt
1   teaspoon prepared mustard
1   teaspoon prepared horseradish

In a large salad bowl combine lettuce, cucumber, kidney beans, turkey salami, carrot, cheese, and green onion.

For dressing, in a small mixing bowl stir together mayonnaise or salad dressing, yogurt, mustard, and horseradish. Pour dressing over salad. Toss lightly to coat. Makes 4 servings.

Nutrition information per serving: 352 calories, 17 g protein, 19 g carbohydrate, 25 g fat (7 g saturated), 50 mg cholesterol, 713 mg sodium, 607 mg potassium.

DUCK SALAD WITH MELON AND CHUTNEY DRESSING

Concerned about fat? Use the turkey option and save about 8 grams of fat per serving.

2 whole boneless domestic duckling
  breasts (about 1½ pounds total)
  or 2 small turkey breast tenderloins
  (about 12 ounces total)
¼ cup chutney
2 tablespoons vinegar
1 tablespoon salad oil
1 tablespoon water
2 teaspoons Dijon-style mustard
2 teaspoons soy sauce
¼ teaspoon crushed red pepper
¼ teaspoon toasted sesame oil
1 clove garlic, minced
6 cups torn mixed greens
2 cups cantaloupe *or* honeydew melon
  chunks
½ cup halved seedless red grapes *or*
  halved pitted dark sweet cherries
¼ cup Spicy Nuts (see recipe, page 140)

Rinse duckling or turkey; pat dry. For duckling, remove skin and fat. Cut each breast in half. Place duckling (meaty side down) or turkey on the unheated rack of a broiler pan. Broil 4 to 5 inches from the heat for 20 to 25 minutes for duckling (12 to 15 minutes for turkey) or till tender and no longer pink, turning once. Cool. Cut duckling or turkey into bite-size strips. Set aside.

Meanwhile, for dressing, in a blender container or food processor bowl combine chutney, vinegar, oil, water, mustard, soy sauce, red pepper, sesame oil, and garlic. Cover and blend or process till nearly smooth. Set dressing aside.

In a large bowl combine torn mixed greens, cantaloupe or honeydew melon chunks, grapes or cherries, and Spicy Nuts. Divide the melon mixture among four salad plates. Arrange duck or turkey strips atop melon mixture. Pour dressing over each serving. Makes 4 servings.

Nutrition information per serving: 470 calories, 20 g protein, 28 g carbohydrate, 33 g fat (5 g saturated), 51 mg cholesterol, 391 mg sodium, 835 mg potassium.

SALMON SALAD WITH JULIENNE VEGETABLES

Looking for a company-special dish? Not only does this broiled salmon salad look impressive, but it also has a sophisticated dressing accented with lemon and fresh herbs.

4   fresh *or* frozen salmon steaks, cut ¾ inch thick (about 1½ pounds)
½   teaspoon finely shredded lemon peel
⅓   cup lemon juice
¼   cup salad oil
2   tablespoons water
2   teaspoons sugar
2   teaspoons snipped fresh thyme *or* ½ teaspoon dried thyme, crushed
2   teaspoons snipped fresh oregano *or* ½ teaspoon dried oregano, crushed
½   teaspoon paprika
⅛   teaspoon pepper
1   clove garlic, minced
2   medium carrots, cut into thin, bite-size strips (about 1¼ cups)
1   medium zucchini, cut into thin, bite-size strips (about 1¼ cups)
1   medium red sweet pepper, cut into thin, bite-size strips (about 1 cup)
¾   cup water
     Boston *or* Bibb lettuce leaves
     Lemon slices (optional)
     Fresh thyme (optional)

Thaw salmon, if frozen. For dressing, in a screw-top jar combine lemon peel, lemon juice, salad oil, the 2 tablespoons water, sugar, thyme, oregano, paprika, pepper, and garlic. Cover and shake well.

Rinse salmon; pat dry with paper towels. Place salmon in a shallow dish. Pour *¼ cup* of the dressing over salmon. Turn salmon once to coat with dressing. Cover and refrigerate for 1 hour, turning salmon once or twice.

Meanwhile, in a medium saucepan combine carrots, zucchini, red sweet pepper, and the ¾ cup water. Bring to boiling. Reduce heat; cover and simmer about 3 minutes or till vegetables are just crisp-tender. Drain vegetables; transfer to a mixing bowl. Pour another *¼ cup* of the dressing over cooked vegetables, tossing lightly to coat. Set vegetables aside. Reserve remaining dressing.

Drain salmon, reserving marinade. Place salmon on the greased unheated rack of a broiler pan. Broil 4 inches from heat for 5 minutes. Using a wide spatula, carefully turn salmon over. Brush with salmon marinade. Broil for 3 to 7 minutes more or till salmon flakes easily with a fork. (Discard any remaining salmon marinade.)

Line four salad plates with lettuce leaves. Arrange marinated vegetables on lettuce leaves. Place salmon steaks on vegetables. Serve with reserved dressing. Garnish each serving with lemon slices and thyme, if desired. Makes 4 servings.

Nutrition information per serving: 326 calories, 26 g protein, 13 g carbohydrate, 20 g fat (3 g saturated), 31 mg cholesterol, 130 mg sodium, 545 mg potassium.

SALMON-PASTA SALAD

Fold the salmon gently into the pasta mixture so it stays in nice big chunks.

1   cup corkscrew macaroni *or* medium
        shell macaroni
1½   cups broccoli flowerets
4   ounces Gruyère *or* Swiss cheese,
        cut into thin, bite-size strips
¼   cup sliced radishes
⅔   cup mayonnaise *or* salad dressing
1   tablespoon snipped fresh basil *or*
        1 teaspoon dried basil, crushed
2   teaspoons white wine Worcestershire
        sauce
⅛   teaspoon garlic salt
1   to 2 tablespoons milk
1   15½-ounce can salmon, chilled
        Leaf lettuce
        Pineapple sage flowers (optional)

In a large saucepan cook pasta in boiling salted water for 9 minutes. Add broccoli; return to boiling. Cook about 4 minutes more or till pasta and broccoli are tender. Drain pasta and broccoli. Rinse with cold water. Drain again.

In a large mixing bowl combine pasta, broccoli, cheese, and radishes.

For dressing, in a small mixing bowl stir together mayonnaise or salad dressing, basil, white wine Worcestershire sauce, garlic salt, and enough milk to make desired consistency. Pour dressing over pasta mixture. Toss lightly to mix. Cover and chill for 4 to 24 hours.

Before serving, if necessary, stir a little additional milk into the pasta mixture to moisten. Drain and flake salmon, discarding skin and bones. Fold salmon into salad mixture.

Divide salmon mixture among four lettuce-lined salad plates. Garnish with pineapple sage flowers, if desired. Makes 4 servings.

Nutrition information per serving: 641 calories, 36 g protein, 19 g carbohydrate, 47 g fat (12 g saturated), 101 mg cholesterol, 999 mg sodium, 686 mg potassium.

LAYERED TUNA AND PASTA SALAD

Be sure to serve this tasty salad in a glass salad bowl with straight sides so you can see all the colorful layers.

1⅓   cups cavatelli *or* medium shell
     macaroni
4   cups shredded iceberg lettuce
1   cup chopped, seeded cucumber
1   cup chopped, seeded tomato
1   9¼-ounce can chunk white tuna
     (water pack), drained and broken
     into chunks *or* 8 ounces flaked,
     cooked tuna
1   cup frozen peas
1   2¼-ounce can sliced ripe olives,
     drained
2   hard-cooked eggs, sliced
2   tablespoons sliced green onion
     Herb Dressing
½   cup finely shredded cheddar *or*
     American cheese (2 ounces)

Cook pasta according to package directions. Drain pasta. Rinse with cold water; drain again.

Place shredded lettuce in the bottom of a 3-quart salad bowl. Layer in the following order: cooked pasta, cucumber, tomato, tuna, peas, olives, egg slices, and green onion.

Carefully spread Herb Dressing evenly over top of salad, sealing to the edge of the bowl. Sprinkle with cheese. Cover tightly with plastic wrap. Chill for 4 to 24 hours. To serve, toss layers together lightly to mix. Makes 6 servings.

Herb Dressing: In a small mixing bowl combine ½ cup *mayonnaise or salad dressing,* ⅓ cup plain *yogurt,* ¼ cup snipped fresh *parsley,* 1 tablespoon snipped fresh *chives,* 1 tablespoon *lemon juice,* 1 tablespoon *Dijon-style mustard,* and ⅛ teaspoon *pepper.* Makes about 1 cup.

Nutrition information per serving: 385 calories, 21 g protein, 27 g carbohydrate, 23 g fat (5 g saturated), 100 mg cholesterol, 407 mg sodium, 423 mg potassium.

GRILLED TUNA SALAD WITH CITRUS-PEPPERCORN VINAIGRETTE

This grilled entree makes a great light and summery supper.

¾ pound fresh *or* frozen tuna *or* swordfish steaks, cut 1 inch thick
Citrus-Peppercorn Vinaigrette
1 cup fresh pea pods *or* ½ of a 6-ounce package frozen pea pods, thawed
6 cups torn Boston *or* Bibb lettuce *or* torn mixed greens
1 cup torn radicchio *or* shredded red cabbage
1 cup sliced fresh mushrooms
1 cup red *or* yellow baby pear tomatoes *or* cherry tomatoes, halved

Thaw fish, if frozen. Rinse fish; pat dry with paper towels. Place fish in a shallow dish. Pour ⅛ *cup* of the Citrus-Peppercorn Vinaigrette over fish. Turn fish once to coat with marinade. Cover and refrigerate for 1 hour, turning fish once or twice.

Meanwhile, if using fresh pea pods, trim ends and remove strings. Cook fresh pea pods in a small amount of boiling water for 1 to 2 minutes or till crisp-tender. Drain; rinse with cold water. (*Do not* cook frozen pea pods.)

In a large mixing bowl combine Boston or Bibb lettuce, radicchio, mushrooms, and pea pods. Set aside.

Drain fish, reserving marinade. Place fish steaks on a greased grill rack. Grill fish on an uncovered grill directly over medium-hot coals for 5 minutes. Using a wide spatula, carefully turn fish over. Brush with marinade. Grill for 3 to 7 minutes more or till fish flakes easily with a fork. Remove fish from grill. Flake fish into bite-size pieces. Discard any remaining marinade.

Add fish to the lettuce mixture. Pour the remaining Citrus-Peppercorn Vinaigrette over lettuce mixture. Toss gently to coat. Serve on salad plates. Garnish with baby pear tomatoes. Makes 4 servings.

Citrus-Peppercorn Vinaigrette: In a screw-top jar combine ½ cup *grapefruit juice,* ⅛ cup *salad oil,* 2 tablespoons snipped fresh *chives,* 2 teaspoons *Dijon-style mustard,* 1 teaspoon *sugar,* and ½ teaspoon *cracked black pepper.* Cover and shake well. Makes about 1 cup.

Nutrition information per serving: 774 calories, 57 g protein, 13 g carbohydrate, 57 g fat (27 g saturated), 155 mg cholesterol, 804 mg sodium, 905 mg potassium.

BLACKENED FISH SALAD

If you use the range-top method for this Cajun specialty, count on your kitchen filling up with smoke! If you don't have an exhaust fan over your range, stick to the grill method.

1 pound fresh *or* frozen catfish, cod, pollack, red snapper, *or* haddock fillets, cut ½ to ¾ inch thick

3 cups torn red-tip leaf lettuce *or* leaf lettuce

3 cups torn spinach

2 medium oranges, peeled and sectioned

1 cup thinly sliced cucumber

1 small red sweet pepper, cut into thin, bite-size strips (½ cup)

3 tablespoons snipped fresh basil *or* 1 teaspoon dried basil, crushed

1½ teaspoons snipped fresh thyme *or* ½ teaspoon dried thyme, crushed

1 teaspoon onion powder

1 teaspoon ground red pepper

1 teaspoon snipped fresh sage *or* ¼ teaspoon ground sage

½ teaspoon garlic salt

½ teaspoon ground white pepper

½ teaspoon ground black pepper

¼ cup margarine *or* butter, melted

⅔ cup Zesty Buttermilk Dressing

Thaw fish, if frozen. Cut into serving-size pieces. In a large salad bowl combine leaf lettuce, spinach, orange sections, cucumber slices, and pepper strips. Divide mixture among four salad plates. Set aside.

Mix basil, thyme, onion powder, ground red pepper, sage, garlic salt, ground white pepper, and ground black pepper. Brush both sides of fish with some of the margarine. Coat both sides with basil mixture.

Remove the rack from a charcoal grill. Place an unoiled 12-inch cast-iron skillet directly on *hot* coals. (If using a gas grill, place skillet on grill rack; turn to high.) Do not position handle over coals. Heat 5 minutes or till a drop of water sizzles.

Add fish to skillet. Carefully drizzle *2 teaspoons* of the margarine over fish. Grill for 2½ to 3 minutes or till blackened. Turn fish; drizzle with another *2 teaspoons* margarine. Grill for 2½ to 3 minutes more or till blackened and fish flakes with a fork. Add fish to salad plates. Serve with Zesty Buttermilk Dressing. Makes 4 servings.

Zesty Buttermilk Dressing: Stir together ⅔ cup *mayonnaise or salad dressing,* ½ cup *buttermilk,* 1 tablespoon snipped fresh or 1 teaspoon crushed dried *basil,* 1 tablespoon snipped fresh *parsley,* ½ teaspoon *seasoned salt,* ¼ teaspoon *garlic powder,* ¼ teaspoon *onion powder,* and ¼ teaspoon *pepper.* Store dressing in the refrigerator. Makes 1¼ cups.

Range-top method: Heat an unoiled 12-inch cast iron over high heat. Brush both sides of fish with melted margarine. Coat both sides with seasoning mixture. Add fish to skillet. Carefully drizzle about *2 teaspoons* of the melted margarine over fish. Cook, uncovered, about 2 minutes or till blackened. Turn fish and drizzle with another *2 teaspoons* of the margarine. Cook for 1½ to 3 minutes more or till blackened and fish flakes easily with a fork. Serve as directed above.

Nutrition information per serving: 247 calories, 22 g protein, 11 g carbohydrate, 14 g fat (3 g saturated), 46 mg cholesterol, 594 mg sodium, 722 mg potassium.

TROPICAL SHRIMP AND FRUIT PLATTER

A spectacular summer salad showcasing tropical fruits, shrimp, and a delicious apricot-sour cream dressing.

½ cup dairy sour cream
¼ cup apricot preserves
2 tablespoons red wine vinegar and oil
    salad dressing
1 tablespoon soy sauce
1 teaspoon prepared mustard
¼ teaspoon ground cinnamon
    Leaf lettuce
1 pound peeled and deveined shrimp,
    cooked and chilled
1 medium papaya, seeded, peeled,
    and sliced
1 medium avocado, pitted, peeled, and
    sliced
1 medium red sweet pepper, cut into
    thin strips
2 cherry tomatoes, halved
½ cup pitted prunes, snipped (optional)
    Ground cinnamon (optional)

For dressing, stir together sour cream, apricot preserves, salad dressing, soy sauce, mustard, and ¼ teaspoon cinnamon. Cover and chill till serving.

Line a large platter with leaf lettuce. Arrange shrimp, papaya, avocado, pepper strips, and cherry tomatoes on the lettuce-lined platter. Garnish with prunes, if desired. Sprinkle dressing with additional cinnamon, if desired. Pass dressing with salad. Makes 4 servings.

Nutrition information per serving: 385 calories, 22 protein, 33 g carbohydrate, 19 g fat (5 g saturated), 187 mg cholesterol, 610 mg sodium, 847 mg potassium.

SHRIMP-STUFFED PAPAYA SALAD

Both the flowers and the leaves of nasturtiums are edible. The bright petals come in yellow, red, and orange and have a peppery, radishlike flavor.

12 to 16 ounces fresh *or* frozen peeled,
         cooked shrimp
½ cup chili sauce
¼ cup sliced green onions
½ teaspoon ground cinnamon
4 to 6 drops bottled hot pepper sauce
     Leaf lettuce
½ cup flaked coconut
2 large papayas, seeded, peeled,
         and halved
4 kiwi fruit, cut into wedges *or*
         2 carambola (star fruit), cut into
         ¼-inch-thick slices
     Nasturtium flowers (optional)

Thaw shrimp, if frozen. Chill well.

Just before serving, in a medium mixing bowl stir together chili sauce, green onions, cinnamon, and hot pepper sauce. Stir in shrimp. Set aside.

Line four salad plates with lettuce leaves. Sprinkle coconut over lettuce. Place a papaya half on each plate. Spoon some of the shrimp mixture into each papaya half. Add kiwi fruit or carambola to plates. Garnish with nasturtium flowers, if desired. Makes 4 servings.

Nutrition information per serving: 400 calories, 22 g protein, 56 g carbohydrate, 10 g fat (8 g saturated), 174 mg cholesterol, 735 mg sodium, 1,018 mg potassium.

SPANISH-STYLE SHRIMP AND RICE SALAD

To bring the look of sunny Spain to your table, line the salad plates with grape leaves instead of lettuce.

1　cup water
1　cup quick-cooking rice
1　teaspoon instant chicken bouillon granules
¼　teaspoon ground turmeric
1　10-ounce package frozen peas with pearl onions
⅓　cup Italian salad dressing
⅛　teaspoon ground red pepper
2　6-ounce packages frozen, peeled, cooked shrimp
　　Leaf lettuce
　　Tomato wedges (optional)

In a small saucepan bring water to boiling. Stir in quick-cooking rice, bouillon granules, and turmeric. Remove from heat. Cover and let stand for 5 minutes.

Meanwhile, cook peas with onions according to package directions. Drain. Stir together rice mixture, peas with onions, salad dressing, and ground red pepper. Add shrimp; toss lightly to coat.

Cover and chill for several hours. Serve on lettuce-lined salad plates. Garnish with tomato wedges, if desired. Makes 4 servings.

Nutrition information per serving: 283 calories, 18 g protein, 28 g carbohydrate, 10 g fat (2 g saturated), 131 mg cholesterol, 550 mg sodium, 247 mg potassium.

SEAFOOD SALAD IN PINEAPPLE BOATS

If fresh pineapple isn't available, use canned pineapple chunks and serve this orange-flavored salad on lettuce-lined plates.

12 ounces fresh *or* frozen sea scallops
4 cups water
1 teaspoon salt
1 large pineapple (about 4½ pounds)
3 cups shredded romaine
1 cup cubed creamy Havarti cheese
    (4 ounces)
1 medium red sweet pepper, cut into
    thin, bite-size strips (1 cup)
1 8-ounce carton plain yogurt
½ teaspoon finely shredded orange peel
1 tablespoon orange juice
1 tablespoon honey
½ teaspoon vanilla
    Orange peel (optional)

Thaw scallops, if frozen. Cut any large scallops in half. In a large saucepan or Dutch oven bring water and salt to boiling. Add scallops. Simmer, uncovered, for 1 to 2 minutes or till scallops are opaque, stirring occasionally. Drain and rinse under cold running water. Cover and chill scallops for 2 to 24 hours.

Use a sharp knife to cut pineapple lengthwise into quarters, crown and all. Remove the hard core from each quarter; discard. Cut out pineapple meat, leaving shells intact. Set shells aside. Remove eyes from pineapple meat. Cut pineapple into chunks, reserving 3 cups (refrigerate remaining pineapple for another use).

In a large mixing bowl combine reserved pineapple chunks, shredded romaine, Havarti cheese, and red sweet pepper. Gently stir in scallops. Spoon salad into pineapple shells.

For dressing, in a small mixing bowl stir together yogurt, finely shredded orange peel, orange juice, honey, and vanilla. Garnish dressing with additional orange peel, if desired. Serve dressing with salad. Makes 4 servings.

Nutrition information per serving: 294 calories, 20 g protein, 26 g carbohydrate, 13 g fat (1 g saturated), 60 mg cholesterol, 371 mg sodium, 649 mg potassium.

CRAB SALAD WITH CURRIED PAPAYA DRESSING

No fresh crabmeat available? Substitute two thawed 8-ounce packages frozen, crab-flavored fish pieces (sometimes called surimi).

½ **pound green beans**
4 **cups shredded Chinese cabbage, romaine,** *or* **iceberg lettuce**
1 **pound cooked lump crabmeat, cut into 1-inch pieces**
1½ **cups sliced strawberries**
1 **papaya, seeded, peeled, and sliced lengthwise**
   Curried Papaya Dressing
   Nasturtium flowers *or* **other edible flowers (optional)**

Wash green beans. Remove ends and strings. In a medium saucepan cook green beans in boiling water about 15 minutes or till just tender. Drain and set aside.

Line four salad plates with shredded Chinese cabbage, romaine, or lettuce. Place crab pieces on the greens. Arrange cooked green beans, strawberries, and papaya slices around the side of each plate. Garnish each salad with nasturtium or other flowers, if desired. Serve with Curried Papaya Dressing. Makes 4 servings.

Curried Papaya Dressing: In a screw-top jar combine ¼ cup *papaya or apricot nectar,* 2 tablespoons *salad oil,* 1 tablespoon snipped fresh *chives,* 1 teaspoon grated *gingerroot,* ½ to 1 teaspoon *curry powder,* ⅛ teaspoon *salt,* and ⅛ teaspoon *pepper.* Cover and shake well.

Nutrition information per serving: 297 calories, 26 g protein, 28 g carbohydrate, 10 g fat (1 g saturated), 113 mg cholesterol, 400 mg sodium, 1,040 mg potassium.

LENTIL-TABBOULEH SALAD

If you like, substitute peanuts for the cashews in this fiber-rich Middle Eastern salad.

1½ cups water
¾ cup dry lentils, rinsed and drained
¾ cup bulgur
¾ cup chopped, seeded cucumber
½ cup snipped fresh parsley
3 tablespoons sliced green onion
⅓ cup olive oil *or* salad oil
⅓ cup lemon juice
1 tablespoon snipped fresh mint *or*
     ½ teaspoon dried mint, crushed
¼ teaspoon salt
¼ teaspoon pepper
1 cup chopped, seeded tomato
¼ cup coarsely chopped cashews
   Cucumber slices (optional)
¼ cup plain yogurt
   Fresh mint sprigs (optional)

In a medium saucepan combine water and lentils. Bring to boiling. Reduce heat; cover and simmer about 30 minutes or till lentils are tender. If all the liquid is not absorbed, drain the lentils.

Rinse bulgur in a colander with cold water. Drain well. In a large mixing bowl combine lentils, bulgur, chopped cucumber, parsley, and green onion. Toss to mix.

For dressing, in a screw-top jar combine oil, lemon juice, mint, salt, and pepper. Cover and shake well. Pour dressing over lentil mixture. Toss lightly to coat. Cover and chill for 4 to 24 hours.

Before serving, stir in chopped tomato and cashews. Garnish with cucumber slices, if desired. Top each serving with 1 tablespoon yogurt. Then garnish with fresh mint, if desired. Makes 4 servings.

Nutrition information per serving: 457 calories, 16 g protein, 52 g carbohydrate, 23 g fat (4 g saturated), 1 mg cholesterol, 472 mg sodium, 926 mg potassium.

GARBANZO BEAN SALAD

Garbanzo beans, the star of this salad, are also known as chick-peas. They have an irregular rounded shape, a nutty taste, and a firm texture.

1 6-ounce jar marinated artichoke
   hearts
2 tablespoon white wine vinegar
1 tablespoon salad oil
1½ teaspoons snipped fresh oregano *or*
   ½ teaspoon dried oregano, crushed
¾ teaspoon dry mustard
1 clove garlic, minced
2 15-ounce cans garbanzo beans, rinsed
   and drained
1 medium zucchini, halved lengthwise
   and sliced (1¼ cups)
1 cup coarsely chopped red *or* green
   sweet pepper
1 cup cubed cheddar cheese (4 ounces)
½ cup sliced pitted ripe olives
   Leaf lettuce

Drain artichoke hearts, reserving marinade. Coarsely chop artichoke hearts; set aside.

For dressing, in a screw-top jar combine reserved artichoke marinade, vinegar, oil, oregano, mustard, and garlic. Cover and shake well. Set dressing aside.

In a large mixing bowl combine garbanzo beans, zucchini, sweet pepper, cheddar cheese, olives, and artichokes. Shake dressing well; pour over bean mixture. Toss lightly to coat. Cover and chill for 2 to 24 hours, stirring occasionally. Serve on lettuce-lined salad plates. Makes 4 to 5 servings.

Nutrition information per serving: 466 calories, 19 g protein, 56 g carbohydrate, 22 g fat (7 g saturated), 30 mg cholesterol, 815 mg sodium, 762 mg potassium.

SOUTH-OF-THE-BORDER BEAN AND PASTA SALAD

For a salad with a little more kick, use Monterey Jack cheese with jalapeño peppers.

1 cup wagon wheel *or* elbow macaroni
1 15-ounce can pinto beans, rinsed
  and drained
1 cup jicama cut into thin, bite-size
  strips
1 cup cubed cheddar *or* Monterey Jack
  cheese (4 ounces)
1 cup chopped, seeded tomato
1 4-ounce can diced green chili peppers,
  drained
2 tablespoons finely chopped onion
  Salsa Dressing
4 cups shredded leaf lettuce
1 to 2 tablespoons milk (optional)
1 medium avocado, seeded, peeled,
  and sliced
  Blue corn tortilla chips *or* tortilla
  chips (optional)

Cook pasta according to package directions. Drain pasta. Rinse with cold water; drain again.

In a large mixing bowl combine pasta, pinto beans, jicama, cheese, tomato, chili peppers, and onion. Toss lightly to mix. Pour Salsa Dressing over pasta mixture. Toss lightly to coat. Cover and chill for 4 to 24 hours.

To serve, divide shredded lettuce among four salad plates. If necessary, stir a little milk into the pasta mixture to moisten. Spoon pasta mixture on shredded lettuce. Arrange sliced avocado on each plate. If desired, garnish each serving with tortilla chips. Makes 4 servings.

Salsa Dressing: In a small mixing bowl stir together ⅓ cup *plain yogurt,* ⅓ cup *mayonnaise or salad dressing,* and 3 tablespoons *salsa.*

Nutrition information per serving: 552 calories, 21 g protein, 47 g carbohydrate, 34 g fat (8 g saturated), 42 mg cholesterol, 823 mg sodium, 957 mg potassium.

TORTELLINI-PESTO SALAD WITH TOMATOES

Use either your own homemade pesto or purchased pesto for this extra-easy, extra-tasty salad.

2   cups frozen *or* refrigerated cheese-
     filled tortellini (about 7 ounces)
1   cup cubed mozzarella cheese
     (4 ounces)
1   cup coarsely chopped, seeded tomato
½   cup purchased *or* homemade pesto
¼   cup pine nuts *or* slivered almonds,
     toasted
     Leaf lettuce
     Fresh basil (optional)

Cook tortellini according to package directions. Drain tortellini. Rinse with cold water; drain again.

In a large mixing bowl combine tortellini, cheese, and chopped tomato. Pour pesto over tortellini mixture. Toss lightly to coat. Cover and chill for 2 to 4 hours.

Just before serving, stir in pine nuts or almonds. Divide pasta mixture among four lettuce-lined plates. Garnish each serving with fresh basil, if desired. Makes 4 servings.

Nutrition information per serving: 360 calories, 21 g protein, 37 g carbohydrate, 15 g fat (4 g saturated), 51 mg cholesterol, 453 mg sodium, 329 mg potassium.

EGG SALAD WITH FRESH VEGGIES

This colorful salad also tastes great in a sandwich. Split 2 small pita bread rounds and line them with lettuce leaves. Each pita will hold about ½ cup of the egg mixture.

8 hard-cooked eggs, chopped
1 small zucchini, quartered lengthwise
     and sliced (1 cup)
½ cup chopped celery
½ cup shredded carrot
2 tablespoons finely chopped green
     onion
2 tablespoons diced pimiento
⅓ cup mayonnaise *or* salad dressing
2 tablespoons creamy Italian *or* creamy
     cucumber salad dressing
1 tablespoon snipped fresh dill *or*
     1 teaspoon dried dillweed
1 teaspoon prepared mustard
⅛ teaspoon salt
   Boston *or* Bibb lettuce leaves
1 to 2 tablespoons milk (optional)

In a medium mixing bowl combine eggs, zucchini, celery, carrot, green onion, and pimiento. Stir in mayonnaise or salad dressing, Italian or cucumber salad dressing, dill, mustard, and salt. Cover and chill for 4 to 24 hours.

To serve, line four salad plates with lettuce leaves. Stir egg mixture gently. If necessary, stir in a little milk to moisten. Divide the egg mixture among the lettuce-lined plates. Makes 4 servings.

Nutrition information per serving: 335 calories, 14 g protein, 7 g carbohydrate, 28 g fat (6 g saturated), 437 mg cholesterol, 399 mg sodium, 404 mg potassium.

TORTELLINI-CAESAR SALAD

This main-dish version of Caesar salad features cheese-filled pasta and a cooked egg dressing in place of the traditional uncooked dressing.

1 egg
⅓ cup chicken broth
3 anchovy fillets, mashed
3 tablespoons olive oil *or* salad oil
2 tablespoons lemon juice
  Few dashes white wine Worcestershire sauce
¾ pound asparagus spears *or* one 10-ounce package frozen cut asparagus
2 cups frozen *or* refrigerated cheese-filled tortellini (about 7 ounces)
1 clove garlic, halved
10 cups torn romaine
½ cup Italian Croutons (see recipe, page 140)
¼ cup finely shredded Parmesan cheese
  Coarsely ground pepper

For dressing, in a blender container or food processor bowl combine egg, chicken broth, anchovy fillets, oil, lemon juice, and Worcestershire sauce. Cover and blend or process till smooth. Transfer dressing to a small saucepan. Cook and stir dressing over low heat for 8 to 10 minutes or till thickened. Do not boil. Transfer to a small bowl. Cover surface with plastic wrap; chill for 2 to 24 hours.

Snap off and discard woody bases from fresh asparagus. If desired, scrape off scales. Break into 1-inch pieces. Cook asparagus, covered, in a small amount of boiling water for 4 to 8 minutes or till tender. (Or, cook frozen asparagus according to package directions.) Cook tortellini according to package directions. Drain; set aside.

To serve, rub the inside of a wooden salad bowl with the cut sides of the garlic clove. Discard garlic clove. Add romaine, asparagus, tortellini, Italian Croutons, and Parmesan cheese to salad bowl. Pour dressing over salad. Toss lightly to mix. Transfer to individual salad plates. Sprinkle pepper over each serving. Makes 4 servings.

Nutrition information per serving: 434 calories, 21 g protein, 42 g carbohydrate, 21 g fat (4 g saturated), 97 mg cholesterol, 711 mg sodium, 690 mg potassium.

WILTED SPINACH WITH APPLES AND FETA CHEESE

For a slightly different look, chop the egg white and then sieve the egg yolk on individual servings of this zesty side salad.

6   cups torn spinach
¼   cup sliced green onions
3   slices bacon
3   tablespoons vinegar
1   teaspoon sugar
¼   teaspoon dry mustard
1   cup sliced *or* chopped apple
⅓   cup crumbled feta cheese
1   hard-cooked egg

In a large mixing bowl combine spinach and green onions. Set aside.

In a 12-inch skillet cook bacon over medium heat till crisp. Remove bacon, reserving *2 tablespoons* drippings in skillet. Drain bacon on paper towels. Crumble bacon and set aside. Carefully stir vinegar, sugar, and mustard into reserved drippings; bring just to boiling.

Add spinach mixture to skillet. Toss for 30 to 60 seconds or till spinach is just wilted. Remove from heat. Add apple and feta cheese. Toss lightly to mix. Transfer to a serving bowl. Remove the yolk from the hard-cooked egg; press yolk through sieve. Chop the egg white. Sprinkle salad with egg yolk and white and crumbled bacon. Serve immediately. Makes 4 servings.

Nutrition information per serving: 143 calories, 9 g protein, 10 g carbohydrate, 9 g fat (4 g saturated), 75 mg cholesterol, 392 mg sodium, 570 mg potassium.

TOSSED VEGETABLE SALAD WITH DILL DRESSING

Make this fresh-tasting, summery salad with a variety of vegetables—try some chopped tomato, red sweet pepper strips, or maybe some sliced radishes.

4   cups mesclun *or* 2 cups torn mixed
        greens and 2 cups torn curly endive
1   cup fresh mushrooms, quartered
1   small yellow summer squash, thinly
        bias-sliced (1 cup)
¾   cup fresh pea pods, ends and strings
        removed and halved crosswise
1   small zucchini
        Dill Dressing
        Fresh dill (optional)

In a large mixing bowl combine mesclun, mushrooms, yellow summer squash, and pea pods. Toss lightly to mix. Divide salad among four salad plates.

Using a vegetable peeler, cut zucchini lengthwise into thin strips; arrange strips on salads. Serve with Dill Dressing. Garnish with fresh dill, if desired. Makes 4 servings.

Dill Dressing: In a small mixing bowl stir together ⅓ cup *mayonnaise or salad dressing,* ¼ cup *plain yogurt,* 1 tablespoon snipped fresh or 1 teaspoon dried *dill,* 1 tablespoon *milk,* ¼ teaspoon *lemon-pepper seasoning,* and dash *garlic powder.*

Nutrition information per serving: 180 calories, 4 g protein, 9 g carbohydrate, 15 g fat (2 g saturated), 12 mg cholesterol, 191 mg sodium, 496 mg potassium.

MIXED GREEN SALAD WITH TOMATO-BASIL VINAIGRETTE

The horseradish in this herb-flavored vinaigrette gives the dressing a robust, tangy flavor.

2 **cups torn spinach**
1 **cup torn Boston** *or* **Bibb lettuce**
1 **cup torn red-tip leaf lettuce**
1 **cup watercress**
1 **cup sliced fresh mushrooms**
   Tomato-Basil Vinaigrette
   Cheese Toasts (see recipe, page 141)

In a large mixing bowl combine spinach, Boston or Bibb lettuce, and red-tip leaf lettuce. Divide greens among four salad plates. Top each salad with watercress and mushrooms. Drizzle Tomato-Basil Vinaigrette over each salad. Serve with Cheese Toasts. Makes 4 servings.

Tomato-Basil Vinaigrette: In a blender container or food processor bowl combine 1 large *tomato,* peeled, seeded, and cut up (¾ cup); 3 tablespoons *salad oil;* 3 tablespoons *red wine vinegar;* 2 tablespoons snipped fresh or 1½ teaspoons dried *basil,* crushed; ½ teaspoon *sugar,* ¼ teaspoon prepared *horseradish;* ⅛ teaspoon *pepper;* and 1 clove *garlic,* minced. Cover and blend or process till smooth. Makes about ¾ cup.

Nutrition information per serving: 152 calories, 4 g protein, 9 g carbohydrate, 12 g fat (2 g saturated), 5 mg cholesterol, 100 mg sodium, 431 mg potassium.

OVERNIGHT VEGETABLE SALAD

Tote this layered salad to your next potluck and toss it just before serving.

4   cups torn mixed greens
1½ cups cauliflower flowerets *and/or*
      broccoli flowerets
1   cup cherry tomatoes, halved
½   of a 6-ounce package frozen pea pods,
      thawed
½   cup sliced radishes
2   hard-cooked eggs, sliced
4   slices bacon, crisp-cooked, drained,
      and crumbled
3   tablespoons sliced green onion
⅓   cup mayonnaise *or* salad dressing
¼   cup dairy sour cream *or* plain yogurt
2   tablespoons grated Parmesan cheese
2   tablespoons purchased pesto
1   to 3 teaspoons milk (optional)
¾   cup shredded cheddar *or* American
      cheese (3 ounces)
    Italian Croutons (optional)
      (see recipe, page 140)

Place greens in the bottom of a 3-quart salad bowl. Layer in the following order: cauliflower or broccoli, cherry tomatoes, pea pods, radishes, hard-cooked eggs, bacon, and green onion.

For dressing, in a small mixing bowl combine mayonnaise or salad dressing, sour cream or yogurt, Parmesan cheese, and pesto. If necessary, stir in milk to make dressing of desired consistency.

Spread dressing evenly over the top of the salad. Sprinkle with cheddar or American cheese. Cover tightly with plastic wrap. Chill for 4 to 24 hours.

To serve, sprinkle with Italian Croutons, if desired. Toss lightly to mix. Makes 6 to 8 servings.

Nutrition information per serving: 292 calories, 11 g protein, 8 g carbohydrate, 25 g fat (7 g saturated), 104 mg cholesterol, 343 mg sodium, 409 mg potassium.

CITRUS TOSSED SALAD WITH CRANBERRY VINAIGRETTE

You can assemble this all-occasion salad several hours ahead of time, but don't add the tangy vinaigrette until just before serving.

4 cups torn mixed greens
1 cup orange sections *and/or* red
    grapefruit sections
1 cup jicama cut into thin, bite-size
    strips
1 small red onion, sliced and separated
    into rings
   Cranberry Vinaigrette
   Italian Croutons (optional)
    (see recipe, page 140)

In a large salad bowl combine torn mixed greens, orange and/or grapefruit sections, jicama, and red onion.

Shake Cranberry Vinaigrette well. Pour over salad. Toss lightly to coat. If desired, top with Italian Croutons. Serve immediately. Makes 4 to 6 servings.

Cranberry Vinaigrette: In a screw-top jar combine ¼ cup *cranberry juice cocktail;* 1 tablespoon *salad oil;* 1 tablespoon *vinegar;* 1 teaspoon snipped fresh or ¼ teaspoon crushed, dried *basil;* and ½ teaspoon *sugar.* Cover and shake well. Makes about ⅓ cup.

Nutrition information per serving: 94 calories, 2 g protein, 15 g carbohydrate, 4 g fat (1 g saturated), 0 mg cholesterol, 6 mg sodium, 250 mg potassium.

STRAWBERRY SPINACH SALAD

For a quick-to-fix main dish, toss ¾ to 1 pound of chopped cooked chicken or turkey with the greens, berries, and asparagus.

1   pound asparagus spears
¼   cup poppy seed *or* Italian salad
     dressing
1   teaspoon finely shredded orange peel
1   tablespoon orange juice
8   cups torn spinach *or* mixed greens
2   cups sliced strawberries *and/or*
     blueberries
¼   cup pecan halves

Snap off and discard woody bases from asparagus. If desired, scrape off scales. Cut asparagus into 1-inch pieces. Cook asparagus, covered, in a small amount of boiling water for 4 to 8 minutes or till crisp-tender; drain. Rinse with cold water. Let asparagus stand in cold water till cool; drain again.

Meanwhile, for dressing, stir together poppy seed or Italian salad dressing, orange peel, and orange juice. Set dressing aside.

In a large salad bowl combine spinach or mixed greens, strawberries or blueberries, and asparagus. Divide salad mixture among four salad plates. Stir dressing again. Drizzle dressing over each salad. Sprinkle with pecans. Makes 4 servings.

Nutrition information per serving: 232 calories, 4 g protein, 14 g carbohydrate, 19 g fat (2 g saturated), 0 mg cholesterol, 321 mg sodium, 795 mg potassium.

CONFETTI BARLEY SALAD

Serve this colorful, vegetable salad alongside grilled pork chops and some sliced tomatoes for a spectacular summertime supper.

1¼ cups water
1 cup quick-cooking barley
¼ cup lime juice
3 tablespoons snipped fresh cilantro
3 tablespoons olive oil *or* salad oil
1 tablespoon water
½ teaspoon salt
⅛ to ¼ teaspoon ground red pepper
1 8¾-ounce can whole kernel corn, drained
½ cup chopped green pepper
½ cup chopped red sweet pepper
3 tablespoons sliced green onion
  Green *or* purple salad savoy leaves

In a medium saucepan combine the 1¼ cups water and barley. Bring to boiling. Reduce heat and simmer, covered, for 10 to 12 minutes or till liquid is absorbed. Cool.

Meanwhile, for dressing, in a screw-top jar combine lime juice, cilantro, oil, the 1 tablespoon water, salt, and ground red pepper. Cover and shake well.

In a large salad bowl combine barley, corn, green pepper, sweet red pepper, and green onion. Shake dressing. Pour dressing over barley mixture; toss lightly to coat. Cover and chill for 4 to 24 hours.

Serve the barley mixture on salad plates lined with salad savoy leaves. Makes 6 servings.

Nutrition information per serving: 212 calories, 5 g protein, 33 g carbohydrate, 8 g fat (1 g saturated), 0 mg cholesterol, 331 mg sodium, 305 mg potassium.

APPLE-CINNAMON FRUIT SLAW
Short on time? Substitute packaged coleslaw mix for the shredded cabbage.

3 cups shredded cabbage
1 cup chopped apple
1 cup seedless red grapes, halved
⅓ cup vanilla yogurt
2 teaspoons milk
⅛ teaspoon ground cinnamon
   Shelled sunflower seeds (optional)

In a large mixing bowl combine cabbage, chopped apple, and grapes.

For dressing, in a small mixing bowl stir together yogurt, milk, and cinnamon. Pour dressing over cabbage mixture. Toss lightly to coat. Cover and chill for 2 to 6 hours. If desired, sprinkle with sunflower seeds just before serving. Makes 4 to 6 servings.

Nutrition information per serving: 81 calories, 2 g protein, 18 g carbohydrate, 1 g fat (0 g saturated), 1 mg cholesterol, 26 mg sodium, 305 mg potassium.

CARIBBEAN SQUASH SALAD

Try other winter squashes, such as acorn, hubbard, or buttercup in this colorful salad.

1 pound butternut squash, peeled, seeded, and cut into ¾-inch pieces (3 cups)
¼ cup orange juice
2 tablespoons snipped fresh cilantro
2 tablespoons salad oil
1 tablespoon finely chopped jalapeño pepper (not seeded)
1 teaspoon sugar
1 cup chopped red sweet pepper
1 cup chopped green pepper
3 tablespoons sliced green onion
   Fresh cilantro (optional)

Cook squash, covered, in a small amount of boiling water for 10 to 15 minutes or till just tender. Drain.

Meanwhile, for dressing, in a screw-top jar combine orange juice, 2 tablespoons cilantro, salad oil, jalapeño pepper, and sugar. Cover and shake well.

In a large mixing bowl combine cooked squash, chopped red sweet pepper, chopped green pepper, and green onion. Toss lightly to mix.

Shake dressing well. Pour over squash mixture; toss lightly to coat. Marinate at room temperature for 2 to 4 hours. Garnish with additional fresh cilantro, if desired. Makes 4 to 6 servings.

Nutrition information per serving: 132 calories, 2 g protein, 18 g carbohydrate, 7 g fat (1 g saturated), 0 mg cholesterol, 6 mg sodium, 458 mg potassium.

SUMMER TOMATO SALAD

Serve this tomato salad, with its basil-buttermilk dressing, along with grilled burgers and potato salad for a consummate, late-summer picnic supper.

Leaf lettuce, curly endive, *and/or*
    other salad greens
4   ripe medium tomatoes, sliced
    Basil Dressing
    Fresh basil (optional)

Line a large serving platter with lettuce, endive, and/or other greens. Arrange tomato slices on greens. Spoon Basil Dressing over tomatoes. Garnish with fresh basil, if desired. Makes 4 servings.

Basil Dressing: In a small mixing bowl combine 2 tablespoons snipped fresh *basil,* 2 tablespoons *buttermilk,* 1 tablespoon sliced *green onion,* and ¼ teaspoon *pepper.* Stir in ¼ cup *mayonnaise or salad dressing.* Cover and chill for 30 minutes before serving.

Nutrition information per serving: 134 calories, 2 g protein, 8 g carbohydrate, 12 g fat (2 g saturated), 8 mg cholesterol, 100 mg sodium, 371 mg potassium.

POTATO SALAD OLÉ

Potato salad takes a south-of-the-border departure in flavor with the addition of taco seasoning mix, corn, and red kidney beans.

3 medium potatoes (1 pound), halved
   lengthwise
¾ cup mayonnaise *or* salad dressing
1 tablespoon taco seasoning mix
1 8-ounce can red kidney beans, rinsed
   and drained
1 8¾-ounce can whole kernel corn,
   drained
½ cup chopped green pepper
½ cup sliced celery
¼ cup sliced pitted ripe olives
   Romaine leaves *or* cabbage leaves
1 small tomato, cut into wedges

In a covered large saucepan cook potatoes in boiling water for 15 to 20 minutes or till just tender; drain well. Cool slightly. Cut potatoes into ¼-inch-thick slices.

Meanwhile, for dressing, in a small mixing bowl combine mayonnaise or salad dressing and taco seasoning mix.

In a large mixing bowl combine kidney beans, corn, chopped green pepper, celery, and olives. Pour dressing over bean mixture. Toss lightly to coat. Add potatoes. Toss lightly again to mix. Cover; chill for 6 to 24 hours.

Serve on romaine- or cabbage-lined salad plates or in a salad bowl. Garnish with tomato wedges. Makes 6 servings.

Nutrition information per serving: 332 calories, 6 g protein, 29 g carbohydrate, 24 g fat (3 g saturated), 16 mg cholesterol, 429 mg sodium, 552 mg potassium.

CARROT SALAD
Crushed pineapple and a touch of orange peel add a new dimension to this classic salad.

3   cups shredded carrot
⅓   cup raisins *or* dried currants
1   8¼-ounce can crushed pineapple,
        well drained
¼   cup mayonnaise *or* salad dressing
1   teaspoon finely shredded orange peel
¼   cup chopped pecans, toasted
        (optional)
     Fresh pineapple slices (optional)

In a large mixing bowl combine shredded carrot and raisins or currants; set aside.

In a small mixing bowl stir together crushed pineapple, mayonnaise or salad dressing, and orange peel. Stir mayonnaise mixture into carrot mixture. Cover and chill for 2 to 24 hours. Sprinkle with toasted pecans and garnish with pineapple slices, if desired. Makes 6 servings.

Nutrition information per serving: 137 calories, 1 g protein, 18 g carbohydrate, 8 g fat (1 g saturated), 5 mg cholesterol, 73 mg sodium, 289 mg potassium.

ORIENTAL WILD RICE SALAD
Serve this festive-looking rice salad with grilled chicken or pork.

¼ cup wild rice
1 cup chicken broth
¼ cup brown rice
3 tablespoons orange juice
2 tablespoons rice vinegar *or* white
  vinegar
1 tablespoon soy sauce
¾ teaspoon toasted sesame oil
½ teaspoon grated gingerroot
1 clove garlic, minced
1 11-ounce can mandarin orange
  sections, drained
1 8-ounce can whole water chestnuts,
  drained and coarsely chopped
½ cup chopped red *or* green sweet
  pepper
2 tablespoons sliced green onion
½ cup frozen peas, thawed
  Spinach leaves
1 tablespoon chopped cashews *or*
  peanuts (optional)
  Tah Tsai flower (optional)

Rinse wild rice in a strainer under cold running water about 1 minute. In a small saucepan combine chicken broth, brown rice, and wild rice. Bring to boiling. Reduce heat and simmer, covered, about 40 minutes or till rice is tender and liquid is absorbed.

Meanwhile, for dressing, in a screw-top jar combine orange juice, rice vinegar or white vinegar, soy sauce, sesame oil, gingerroot, and garlic. Cover and shake well.

In a large mixing bowl combine cooked rice, mandarin orange sections, water chestnuts, sweet pepper, and green onion. Pour dressing over rice mixture. Toss lightly to coat. Cover and chill for 4 to 24 hours. Just before serving, stir in peas.

Serve salad on spinach-lined plates. Sprinkle each serving with cashews or peanuts and garnish with a Tah Tsai flower, if desired. Makes 4 servings.

Nutrition information per serving: 178 calories, 7 g protein, 34 g carbohydrate, 2 g fat (0 g saturated), 0 mg cholesterol, 496 mg sodium, 513 mg potassium.

FRESH FRUIT SALAD WITH YOGURT DRESSING

Any fresh fruit combination would go great with this lemon-flavored yogurt dressing.

Salad savoy leaves
2   cups cantaloupe *and/or* honeydew
      melon balls
2   cups red raspberries *and/or*
      blackberries
1   cup sliced, peeled kiwi fruit
1   cup halved strawberries
1   cup sliced carambola (star fruit)
      (optional)
    Lemon Yogurt Dressing
3   tablespoons chopped pecans *or*
      walnuts, toasted
    Fresh mint (optional)

Line a serving platter with salad savoy leaves. Arrange cantaloupe or honeydew melon balls, red raspberries or blackberries, sliced kiwi fruit, halved strawberries, and, if desired, sliced carambola on savoy leaves. Drizzle with Yogurt Dressing. Sprinkle salad with nuts. Garnish with fresh mint, if desired. Makes 6 servings.

Lemon Yogurt Dressing: In a small mixing bowl stir together one 8-ounce carton *vanilla yogurt,* 2 tablespoons *mayonnaise or salad dressing,* and ½ teaspoon finely shredded *lemon peel.* Cover and chill till serving. Makes 1 cup.

Nutrition information per serving: 294 calories, 6 g protein, 33 g carbohydrate, 18 g fat (2 g saturated), 5 mg cholesterol, 68 mg sodium, 759 mg potassium.

AVOCADO AND PAPAYA SALAD

If your papaya isn't ripe when you buy it, let it stand at room temperature for 3 to 5 days until it's mostly yellow to yellowish brown. To speed the ripening of your avocado, put it in a paper bag for a day or two.

2   tablespoons walnut oil *or* salad oil
2   tablespoons raspberry vinegar
   Boston *or* Bibb lettuce leaves
2   medium grapefruit, peeled and sectioned
1   medium avocado, pitted, peeled, and cubed *or* sliced
1   medium papaya, seeded, peeled, and sliced
   Pansies *or* other edible flowers (optional)

For dressing, in a screw-top jar combine walnut oil or salad oil and raspberry vinegar. Cover and shake well.

Line four salad plates with lettuce leaves. Arrange grapefruit sections, avocado cubes or slices, and papaya slices on lettuce-lined plates. Shake dressing well. Drizzle over each salad. Garnish with pansies or other edible flowers, if desired. Makes 4 servings.

Nutrition information per serving: 215 calories, 2 g protein, 20 g carbohydrate, 15 g fat (1 g saturated), 0 mg cholesterol, 13 mg sodium, 693 mg potassium.

CRANBERRY-WALDORF SALAD

Here's a little tip from our Test Kitchen: spray your kitchen scissors with nonstick spray coating before snipping the dates and the scissors won't get sticky!

2   cups chopped pears *or* chopped apples
½   cup seedless grapes, halved
½   cup sliced celery
⅓   cup slivered almonds *or* broken
    pecans, toasted
¼   cup snipped pitted whole dates *or*
    raisins
    Leaf lettuce
⅓   cup whole cranberry sauce
2   tablespoons mayonnaise *or* salad
    dressing
2   tablespoons dairy sour cream
2   tablespoons milk
1   teaspoon lemon juice
⅛   teaspoon celery seed

In a medium mixing bowl combine chopped pears or apples, grapes, celery, almonds or pecans, and dates or raisins. Divide fruit mixture among four lettuce-lined salad plates.

For dressing, in a small mixing bowl combine cranberry sauce, mayonnaise or salad dressing, sour cream, milk, lemon juice, and celery seed. Drizzle dressing over fruit mixture. Makes 4 to 6 servings.

Nutrition information per serving: 266 calories, 4 g protein, 37 g carbohydrate, 13 g fat (2 g saturated), 8 mg cholesterol, 70 mg sodium, 400 mg potassium.

SPICY NUTS

These tantalizing nuts are seasoned with a touch of ground red pepper and cumin.

¾ **cup broken walnuts** *or* **pecans**
1 **tablespoon margarine** *or* **butter, softened**
¼ **teaspoon ground red pepper**
¼ **teaspoon ground cumin**
   Dash salt

Combine walnuts or pecans, margarine or butter, red pepper, cumin, and salt. Spread nuts in a single layer in a shallow baking pan.

Bake in a 350° oven about 10 minutes or till light brown, stirring once or twice. Cool.

To store, place in an airtight container and refrigerate for up to 1 month. Bring to room temperature before serving. Makes ¾ cup.

Nutrition information per ¼ cup serving: 228 calories, 4 g protein, 6 g carbohydrate, 22 g fat (2 g saturated), 0 mg cholesterol, 96 mg sodium, 162 mg potassium.

ITALIAN CROUTONS

Use these homemade croutons to dress up any salad.

¼ **cup margarine** *or* **butter**
3 **tablespoons grated Parmesan cheese**
½ **teaspoon dried Italian seasoning, crushed**
⅛ **teaspoon garlic powder**
4 **½-inch-thick slices French bread, cut into ¾-inch cubes**

In a large skillet melt margarine or butter. Remove from heat. Stir in Parmesan cheese, Italian seasoning, and garlic powder. Add bread cubes, stirring till cubes are coated.

Spread bread cubes in a single layer in a shallow baking pan. Bake in a 300° oven for 10 minutes; stir. Bake for 5 to 10 minutes more or till bread cubes are dry and crisp. Cool completely before using.

To store, place in an airtight container and store in the refrigerator for up to 1 month. Bring to room temperature before serving. Makes about 2 cups.

Nutrition information per 2 tablespoon serving: 56 calories, 1 g protein, 4 g carbohydrate, 4 g fat (1 g saturated), 1 mg cholesterol, 106 mg sodium, 11 mg potassium.

CHEESE TOASTS

If Brie is your cheese choice for these delicious rounds, trim off the white rind before spreading the cheese on the bread.

1 **French-style roll (about 6 inches long) bias-sliced ½-inch-thick (6 to 8 slices)**
3 **ounces Brie cheese, soft goat cheese, *or* crumbled blue cheese**

Arrange bread slices on the rack of an unheated broiler pan. Broil 4 to 5 inches from the heat about 1 minute on each side or till toasted.

Spread cheese over each slice of toasted bread. (If using Brie cheese, remove the rind.) Watching carefully, broil 4 to 5 inches from the heat for 1 to 2 minutes or till cheese is heated through. Serve immediately. Makes 6 to 8 rounds.

Nutrition information per round: 100 calories, 5 g protein, 10 g carbohydrate, 5 g fat (3 g saturated), 14 mg cholesterol, 193 mg sodium, 38 mg potassium.

CHOOSE EDIBLE FLOWERS WITH CARE

The best edible flowers are unsprayed blossoms from your own garden. Edible flowers also can be obtained from the produce section of some supermarkets, local herb gardens, some restaurant or produce suppliers, and mail-order outlets. Not all flowers and not all parts of all flowering plants are edible. Choose only those specified below or ones you know to be safe. Use flowers that have been grown without the use of pesticides or other chemicals. Do not use flowers from florist shops—they're usually treated with chemicals. Flowers safe to eat: chive blossoms, nasturtiums, pansies, violets and violas, rose petals, calendulas, geraniums, daylilies, dianthus, borage, and marigolds.

Keep track of your daily nutrition needs by using the information we provide at the end of each recipe. We've analyzed the nutritional content of each recipe serving for you. When a recipe gives an ingredient substitution, we used the first choice in the analysis. If it makes a range of servings (such as 4 to 6), we used the smallest number. Ingredients listed as optional weren't included in the calculations.

METRIC COOKING HINTS

By making a few conversions, cooks in Australia, Canada, and the United Kingdom can use the recipes in Better Homes and Gardens® *Salads* with confidence. The charts on this page provide a guide for converting measurements from the U.S. customary system, which is used throughout this book, to the imperial and metric systems. There also is a conversion table for oven temperatures to accommodate the differences in oven calibrations.

Volume and Weight: Americans traditionally use cup measures for liquid and solid ingredients. The chart (top right) shows the approximate imperial and metric equivalents. If you are accustomed to weighing solid ingredients, here are some helpful approximate equivalents.

■ 1 cup butter, caster sugar, or rice = 8 ounces = about 250 grams
■ 1 cup flour = 4 ounces = about 125 grams
■ 1 cup icing sugar = 5 ounces = about 150 grams

Spoon measures are used for smaller amounts of ingredients. Although the size of the tablespoon varies slightly among countries. However, for practical purposes and for recipes in this book, a straight substitution is all that's necessary.

Measurements made using cups or spoons should always be level, unless stated otherwise.

Product Differences: Most of the ingredients called for in the recipes in this book are available in English-speaking countries. However, some are known by different names. Here are some common American ingredients and their possible counterparts:

■ Sugar is granulated or caster sugar.
■ Powdered sugar is icing sugar.
■ All-purpose flour is plain household flour or white flour. When self-rising flour is used in place of all-purpose flour in a recipe that calls for leavening, omit the leavening agent (baking soda or baking powder) and salt.
■ Light corn syrup is golden syrup.
■ Cornstarch is cornflour.
■ Baking soda is bicarbonate of soda.
■ Vanilla is vanilla essence.

USEFUL EQUIVALENTS

⅛ teaspoon = 0.5ml
¼ teaspoon = 1ml
½ teaspoon = 2 ml
1 teaspoon = 5 ml
¼ cup = 2 fluid ounces = 50ml
⅓ cup = 3 fluid ounces = 75ml
½ cup = 4 fluid ounces = 125ml

⅔ cup = 5 fluid ounces = 150ml
¾ cup = 6 fluid ounces = 175ml
1 cup = 8 fluid ounces = 250ml
2 cups = 1 pint
2 pints = 1 litre
½ inch =1 centimetre
1 inch = 2 centimetres

BAKING PAN SIZES

American	Metric
8x1½-inch round baking pan	20x4-centimetre sandwich or cake tin
9x1½-inch round baking pan	23x3.5-centimetre sandwich or cake tin
11x7x1½-inch baking pan	28x18x4-centimetre baking pan
13x9x2-inch baking pan	32.5x23x5-centimetre baking pan
2-quart rectangular baking dish	30x19x5-centimetre baking pan
15x10x1-inch baking pan	38x25.5x2.5-centimetre baking pan (Swiss roll tin)
9-inch pie plate	22x4- or 23x4-centimetre pie plate
7- or 8-inch springform pan	18- or 20-centimetre springform or loose-bottom cake tin
9x5x3-inch loaf pan	23x13x6-centimetre or 2-pound narrow loaf pan or paté tin
1½-quart casserole	1.5-litre casserole
2-quart casserole	2-litre casserole

OVEN TEMPERATURE EQUIVALENTS

Fahrenheit Setting	Celsius Setting*	Gas Setting
300°F	150°C	Gas Mark 2
325°F	160°C	Gas Mark 3
350°F	180°C	Gas Mark 4
375°F	190°C	Gas Mark 5
400°F	200°C	Gas Mark 6
425°F	220°C	Gas Mark 7
450°F	230°C	Gas Mark 8
Broil		Grill

Electric and gas ovens may be calibrated using Celsius. However, increase the Celsius setting 10 to 20 degrees when cooking above 160°C with an electric oven. For convection or forced-air ovens (gas or electric), lower the temperature setting 10°C when cooking at all heat levels.